# HISTORY OF LEHIGH VALLEY TRANSIT COMPANY

EDITOR — Randolph L. Kulp

## Contributors

Robert H. Adams, Jr., Platteville, Wisconsi
Clinton T. Andrews, West Palm Beach, Florida
Frederick E. Barber, Allentown, Pennsylvania
John J. Bowman, Jr., Lancaster, Pennsylvania
E. Everett Edwards, Birmingham, Michigan
Harold Forsyth Collection
Earl R. Gerber, Bethlehem, Pennsylvania
Francis J. Goldsmith, Jr., Flushing, New York
Daniel P. Grimes, Reading, Pennsylvania
Charles W. Houser, Sr., Allentown, Pennsylvania
Frederick James, Easton, Pennsylvania
Howard E. Johnston Collection
Orville S. Kulp, Allentown, Pennsylvania
Randolph L. Kulp, Allentown, Pennsylvania
Andrew W. Maginnis, Philadelphia, Pennsylvania

Stephen D. Maguire, Belmar, New Jersey
Elwood C. McEllroy, Allentown, Pennsylvania
William D. Middleton, San Francisco, Calif.
Roy Miller, Allentown, Pennsylvania
James H. Richards, Holland, Pennsylvania
William J. Rugen, Richmond Hill, New York
Gerhard Salomon, Allentown, Pennsylvania
Industrial Photo Service, Albany, New York
John P. Scharle, Allentown, Pennsylvania
Fred Schneider III, Lancaster, Pennsylvania
Alma S. Sell, Allentown, Pennsylvania
Howard P. Sell Collection
James P. Shuman, New York, New York
Lester K. Wismer, Souderton, Pennsylvania
Rev. Samuel P. Worthington, Bloomington, Indiana

April 1, 1966
Lehigh Valley Chapter
National Railway Historical Society, Incorporated
Allentown, Pennsylvania

OFFICERS — LEHIGH VALLEY CHAPTER, N. R. H. S.

> President — Elwood C. McEllroy
> 1st Vice President — William T. Coe
> 2nd Vice President — Joseph W. Reinbold
> 3rd Vice President — Ralph M. Steinmetz
> Secretary — Gerhard Salomon
> Treasurer — Ernest Kovacs
> Chapter Director — Frank W. Bergwall
> Editor — Randolph L. Kulp

COVER DESIGNER — William T. Coe

PRINTER — A B C Printing & Photo-Offset, Bethlehem, Pa.

Lehigh Valley Chapter, National Railway Historical Society, Incorporated, dedicates this history to —

The Employees of Lehigh Valley Transit Company of Allentown, Pennsylvania, whose combined efforts produced an electric railway operation which equalled that of any offered in the United States.

**WILDSIDE PRESS**

# PREFACE

Few electric street railway systems located in eastern United States, perhaps in the entire nation, gained the respect and admiration which the public bestowed upon Lehigh Valley Transit Company of Allentown, Pennsylvania. During the many years of electric railway operation the patrons recognized the system as an efficient dependable transportation medium. Officials of the company, fully aware of their responsibilities to the public, organized convenient service and purchased modern equipment whenever conditions warranted; crew members safely and properly maintained established schedules to the best of their ability; and shop workers produced an unexcelled quality of craftsmanship. Out-of-town business men who visited local marts generally regarded the transit company's service as superior to that of other areas.

Lehigh Valley Transit Company and its predecessor organizations developed a colorful history. Commencing with the post-Civil War period public street railway operations in Allentown expanded progressively from a three and one-half mile horse car system into an electric railway property which totalled slightly less than two hundred miles of first class right of way at its peak in 1920. A variety of schedules provided excellent accommodations to many hamlets, villages, towns, and cities located in eastern Pennsylvania and a portion of northwestern New Jersey. During eighty-three years of street railway service the various railway companies operated approximately seven hundred cars of various types which ranged from the bouncing single truck wooden car to the luxurious double truck high speed aluminum interurban car.

Since most records of the individual companies which formed Lehigh Valley Transit Company have been destroyed, this book represents a blending of data gleaned from microfilm records filed in the library of Call-Chronicle Newspapers, Incorporated; discussions with a host of personnel attached to Lehigh Valley Transit Company's operating, maintenance, and official staffs; various county and municipal histories; sundry trade and financial periodicals; and notes diligently recorded by many electric railway enthusiasts. In instances where actual dates have been elusive an estimated date has been inserted so that an event can be identified as nearly as possible in its proper chronological sequence.

Basically, the text presents a compact narrative arranged for perusal by the layman rather than the technician. The editor of this publication believes that readers prefer a text based on the flow of outstanding events rather than a maze of technical and financial data; a series of intricate legal and corporate maneuvers; detailed physical alterations and frequent operational and schedule adjustments; and facts generally considered to be of minor interest. There is no doubt that lengthy volumes could be written about the transit system and predecessor organizations. As a convenience to readers the text briefly and individually traces the development of the transit company's three divisions — Allentown, Philadelphia, and Easton. Duplication of information pertaining to all three divisions has been held to a minimum, and basic facts applicable to all three divisions have been generally included with Allentown Division's history.

Photographs which accompany each division's history represent the most appropriate which could be gathered for this publication. The reader should bear in mind that no single comprehensive source of street railway photographs exists anywhere in the Lehigh Valley area for reproduction in this or any other publication. Most of the scenes presented herein have been gleaned from the private collections of electric railway historians. Photographs have been arranged chronologically, and informative technical data has been inserted underneath the caption. Contributors of both photographs and historical data are again credited with the photograph contributed.

This booklet represents the eighth historical publication composed and presented by the members of Lehigh Valley Chapter, National Railway Historical Society, Incorporated, since the publication of historical booklets was inaugurated in 1955. Actually, this rendition has been prepared to commemorate the chapter's twenty-fifth anniversary of its founding and accomplishes the main project as established in the organizational meeting held in May, 1941.
April 1, 1966

Editor
Randolph L. Kulp
602 St. John St.
Allentown, Penna. 18103

# LEHIGH VALLEY TRANSIT COMPANY
## ALLENTOWN DIVISION

### HORSE CAR OPERATIONS

Allentown Passenger Railway Company, a horse car system, inaugurated public railway service along three and one-half miles of Allentown's streets on May 21, 1868, with five cars and twelve horses. The railway company's western terminus and headquarters had been established behind Black Bear Hotel situated on the northeast corner of Ninth and Hamilton streets intersection. Single trackage followed Hamilton Street eastward to Second Street but circumvented Hamilton Street hill via South Fifth, Walnut, and South Fourth streets. At Second and Hamilton streets intersection one branch continued eastward across Lehigh River and terminated at the passenger station of Lehigh and Susquehanna Railroad Company (operated by The Central Railroad Company of New Jersey effective 1871) located eastward from the canal and southward from the bridge. Another branch extended southward from Hamilton Street along Second Street, passed Lehigh Valley Railroad Company's original passenger station, located near Union Street, and terminated at East Pennsylvania Railroad Company's (Reading Company) original passenger station and engine terminal located at East Penn Junction. The main route continued northward through Sixth Ward via Second, Linden, Ridge (Avenue), Gordon and Front streets to a terminus at Allentown Furnace located northward from Tilghman Street and westward from Lehigh Valley Railroad Company's main line. Conveniently located turnouts permitted the passing of cars.

During 1889 the railway company improved facilities and extended trackage by means of various projects: formed a loop through the heart of Allentown by constructing trackage westward along Hamilton Street from Ninth Street to Tenth Street and along North Tenth, Gordon, North Ninth, Allen, and North Seventh streets back to Hamilton Street to a wye junction with existing trackage at Center Square; when Lehigh County Agricultural Society moved the fairgrounds from North Sixth and Chew streets to North Seventeenth and Chew streets, built trackage to the tract from Tenth and Hamilton streets intersection via Hamilton, North Madison, Gordon, and North Seventeenth streets; built an office and more adequate stables and carbarn along the east side of North Madison Street between Chew and Gordon streets; installed track on Hamilton Street hill and discontinued use of trackage on South Fifth, Walnut, and South Fourth streets; and revised the Allentown Furnace route by constructing track on Ridge Avenue from Gordon to Tilghman Street and on Tilghman Street from Ridge Avenue to Front Street in place of track originally built along Gordon and Front streets.

Construction and opening of Lehigh Valley Railroad Company's new passenger station near Fourth and Hamilton streets intersection and Allentown Terminal Railroad Company's passenger station at Race and Hamilton streets intersection early in 1890 caused abandonment of all trackage extending eastward along Hamilton Street from a point near Second Street and southward along Second Street from Hamilton Street.

The horse car railway operated a variety of small four-wheel closed cars designed with open platforms until manufacturers produced open "summer" cars in 1889. Lack of heating systems in closed cars during winter operations posed no problem for the horse car company — clean straw

An eastbound horse car of Allentown Passenger Railway Company moves along Hamilton Street towards 5th Street in Allentown during a snow storm, circa 1871.

Westbound car No. 3, drawn by two horses, engulfed in crowd at 7th and Hamilton Streets, Allentown, circa 1890.

strewn over the floor provided warmth for passengers' feet. The driver braved raw cold winds and precipitation from his position on the open platform, but the conductor sought shelter inside the car after performing his chores on the rear platform. One man cars, for which the driver also served as conductor, operated several daily schedules between Allentown's business district and the railroad stations.

## ELECTRIC SERVICE INTRODUCED

Adaptation of electricity to street railway operations found Allentown among the early entries. Horse car service ended on April 17, 1891, and Allentown and Bethlehem Rapid Transit Company, successor to Allentown Passenger Railway Company, hurriedly laid either new single or double standard gauge track and strung overhead wire on most streets served by the horse car system; completely abandoned the 7th and 10th Street loop; removed trackage on North Madison Street between Hamilton and Chew streets; laid new electric track on North Twelfth Street between Hamilton and Chew streets and on Chew Street between North Twelfth Street and a connection with original right of way at Madison Street; converted the stables located on Madison Street into a carbarn; purchased a variety of single truck open and closed cars (numbered consecutively); and installed and operated temporary power producing machinery in Allentown Steam Heating And Power Company's plant located near South Hall and Hamilton streets until completion of the new powerhouse at Front and Linden streets on September 28, 1891. The new electric railway company had been organized by financiers from Boston, Massachusetts.

Allentown and Bethlehem Rapid Transit Company inaugurated electric car service with tan and cream painted open-type cars in Allentown along Hamilton Street on July 1, 1891. Service from Allentown reached Rittersville via Allentown-Bethlehem pike (Hanover Avenue) July 27, 1891; Broad and New streets, Bethlehem, via Broad Street, August 2, 1891; Bethlehem Fair Grounds, Elizabeth Avenue and Linden Street, via Linden Street, September 10, 1891; West Catasauqua via Sixth Ward and Fullerton, September 2, 1891, but horse cars operated in Catasauqua along Front Street pending construction of a new bridge across Lehigh River at Race Street; South Bethlehem from Bethlehem, May 31, 1892; and after completion of a new bridge, West Catasauqua to Catasauqua, September 6, 1892. Trackage from Bethlehem to South Bethlehem followed New Street from Broad Street to Fourth Street; Fourth Street from New Street to Wyandotte Street, Wyandotte Street from Fourth Street to Broadway; and along Broadway from Wyandotte Street to a terminus located at the Fountain Hill-South Bethlehem boundary line near Fiot Street. A spur also extended along Second Street in South Bethlehem from New Street to Union Station maintained jointly by Philadelphia and Reading Railway Company and Lehigh Valley Railroad Company, and trackage built from Broad Street to New Street via Main and Church streets established additional service in Bethlehem's business district. White bands painted on power line poles identified stopping points for electric cars and a manually operated signal system governed movements over single track routes between sidings and junctions.

The railway company provided more service in Allentown with the construction of trackage along North Seventh Street between Hamilton Street and Washington Street on April 30, 1892, and westward from 12th Street via Hamilton and North Seventeenth streets to a connection with the terminus of original trackage located at North Seventeenth and Chew streets intersection on August 1, 1893.

7

Westbound summer car No. 1 of Allentown and Bethlehem Rapid Transit Company stands at 7th and Hamilton Streets intersection on first day of electric railway operations in Allentown, July 1, 1891.
(Nos. 1-11, Briggs, 1891)

Bethlehem-bound car No. 4, carrying company officials, stands before Rittersville Hotel during Allentown-Bethlehem inaugural trip, August 2, 1891.

During winter months closed cars with open platforms replaced open cars on all routes. The motorman, muffled in a heavy overcoat, met the onslaught of winter weather as he laboriously wound the controller handle and mechanical hand brake and clanged the foot gong from his position behind an unprotected dash board while the conductor performed his duties inside the car. In 1899 a city ordinance outlawed the use of open platform cars during winter months. Accordingly, carpenters employed by the traction company created a vestibule by constructing protruding windows and frames, protruding to allow cranking of the brake handle, between the top of the dash board and roof tip. Some, but not all, vestibules included folding side doors. Thereafter, car manufacturers produced closed cars with enclosed platforms. Variously painted colored destination signs fastened on either the roof or the dash board indicated direction during day time operations and for night time accommodations red marker lights fastened on the front end indicated Bethlehem-bound and green indicated Catasauqua-bound cars. Coal stoves, located along one side of the cars' center, provided warmth for passengers during winter operations and electric lamps fastened to the ceiling offered adequate interior illumination after dusk. Installation of protective fenders, or "cow catchers", to the bumper and dash board reduced serious accidents involving pedestrians and animals.

Construction of Rittersville Carbarn, the first of several additional structures built by the electric railway companies, commenced on May 2, 1892. During summer, 1893, southward and across the highway from the carbarn, the company established a menagerie and merry-go-round in a wooded tract which received the identification as Central Park. Northward from the park and eastward from the carbarn the electric railway company built a horse racing track. When attendance and enthusiasm for racing diminished, the electric railway company converted the race track into a baseball diamond. After World War I an automobile parking lot and semi-real estate development replaced the baseball diamond and adjoining land. Facilities within Central Park and corresponding attendance, however, expanded tremendously to the extent that by 1910 it had become Lehigh Valley area's main summer amusement center.

## ELECTRIC RAILWAY EMPIRE PROPOSED

Allentown and the Lehigh Valley area became a traction battleground after Albert L. Johnson arrived in Allentown from Cleveland, Ohio, early in 1893, and organized Allentown and Lehigh Valley Traction Company. Mr. Johnson, as president of the new organization, vigorously challenged Allentown and Bethlehem Rapid Transit Company's monopoly of electric railway service and eventually emerged victorious.

Allentown and Lehigh Valley Traction Company built a two story carbarn, powerhouse, and office on Lehigh Creek's right bank eastward from Lehigh Street in Salisbury Township near Allentown's boundary and inaugurated Allentown-West Catasauqua service via Steckel's Hill and Fullerton on October 14, 1893, and Allentown-South Bethlehem service via Aineyville, Salisbury Township's rural area, Gauffs Hill, and Fountain Hill on January 22, 1894. Standard gauge trackage followed Lehigh, Union, South Sixth, North Sixth, Washington and North Fourth streets through Allentown. In South Bethlehem trackage followed Seneca, Freytag, Cherokee, Dakotah, Broadway, and Broadhead (Avenue) streets to a terminus at Third Street and eastward to another terminus located at Fourth and Hill streets via a circuitous route which followed Brodhead (Avenue), Packer (Avenue), New, and Fourth

Howard P. Sell Collection

Bethlehem-bound car No. 43 of Allentown and Bethlehem Rapid
Transit Company stands on Hamilton Street near 12th Street, circa 1893.
(Nos. 40-43, Newburyport, 1892)

Howard P. Sell Collection

Allentown and Lehigh Valley Traction Company car No. 28, bound
for Allentown, stands in South Bethlehem on Broadway near Brodhead
Avenue after completing Allentown-South Bethlehem inaugural trip, January 22, 1894.
(Nos. 21-28, Brill, 1893)

streets. The system's bulky buff and cream painted single end closed cars, later nicknamed "gun boats", required the construction of a turntable at each terminus.

Mr. Johnson acquired controlling shares of Allentown and Bethlehem Rapid Transit Company on February 28, 1894, and all stock by July 15, 1895. Installation of switches at Sixth and Hamilton streets in Allentown's business district physically connected trackage of the former competitors and thereby established the intersection as the traction center in Allentown. New trackage construction along Fiot Street from Seneca Street to Broadway connected both systems in South Bethlehem and caused abandonment of all other trackage which Allentown and Lehigh Valley Traction Company had originally built in the borough. Another junction constructed in West Catasauqua also connected both systems. As the result of the merger, Allentown and Lehigh Valley Traction Company acquired sixty-one passenger cars of various types; a few utility cars; and the carbarn, yard, and repair shop facilities located along North Madison Street. Although electric railway passenger schedules and utility cars operated from both North Madison Street and South Allentown carbarns, the traction company regarded South Allentown Carbarn as the center of operations.

Under Mr. Johnson's efficient direction electric railway trackage expanded into all sections of the Lehigh River valley except that lying westward. Electric car service reached Coplay from Catasauqua, June 23, 1894; Siegfried (Northampton) from Catasauqua, October 23, 1894; Hellertown from Bethlehem, December 9, 1897; Rentzheimer's Cave from Hellertown (operated for a short duration), July 27, 1898; Emaus (later Emmaus) from Aineyville in Salisbury Township, September 17, 1898; Macungie from Emaus, August 29, 1899; establishment of Fullerton Junction by connecting both original routes to West Catasauqua with new trackage construction and abandonment of the eastern, or lower, route between Fullerton and West Catasauqua, November 1, 1899; Egypt from Coplay, August 9, 1900; Slatington from Allentown, November 4, 1900; Freemansburg from Northampton Heights, Bethlehem, October 30, 1901; and Slatedale from Slatington, 1902. In Allentown the construction of new trackage on Washington Street commencing April 5, 1899, connected track on North Sixth and North Seventh streets and established additional service to North Allentown, and on September 10, 1900, track crews constructed track along North Twelfth Street between Chew and Gordon streets and on Gordon Street between North Madison and North Twelfth streets and removed track on Chew Street between North Twelfth Street and North Madison Street and along North Madison Street as far as the carbarn.

Effective November 17, 1899, Mr. Johnson reorganized his electric railway holdings under the control of Lehigh Valley Traction Company. In addition, leased independent connecting companies further increased his influence over Lehigh Valley area electric railways: Bethlehem and Nazareth Street Railway Company, opened October 3, 1899, leased January 27, 1900; Easton Consolidated Electric Company, organized May 19, 1899, as operators of all Easton, Pennsylvania and Phillipsburg, New Jersey, city and suburban traction companies, the Lafayette Traction Company, the oldest of the group having commenced operation on January 14, 1888, leased January 27, 1900; and Slate Belt Electric Railway Company, opened November 14, 1900, from Bangor through Pen Argyl, Wind Gap, Belfast, to Nazareth, leased December 1, 1900. Lease arrangements with the various traction companies included rolling stock as well as

Siegfrieds-bound car No. 101 of Allentown and Lehigh Valley Traction Company stands on original right of way near Fullerton, circa 1896. (Nos. 100-109, Stephenson, 1894)

Bethlehem-bound Lehigh Valley Traction Company car No. 74 and crew pose for photograph along Allentown-Bethlehem Pike (Hanover Avenue), circa 1898. (No. 74, Stephenson, 1891; ex A&BRT No. 23)

trackage and carbarns and, as a result, several cars received identification of Lehigh Valley Traction Company and Easton Transit Company.

Mr. Johnson, after consolidating the routes of independent local street railway companies with his organization, planned two lengthy connecting interurban routes which would have operated in co-ordination with the trackage located in the Lehigh River valley. One route extended from Allentown to Philadelphia and the other from Philadelphia to New York. Accordingly, Lehigh Valley Traction Company ordered thirty-five heavy double truck wooden body deck roof interurban railway cars from St. Louis Car Company, St. Louis, Missouri, on January 10, 1901, for standard gauge routes which extended from Allentown to Bethlehem, Easton, Bangor, Slatington, Siegfried, Hellertown and Macungie and towns enroute and on January 18, 1901, forty cars for wide gauge (5 ft., 2½ in.) trackage planned for Philadelphia and New York divisions. The traction company identified standard gauge cars with consecutive numbering, in relation to the roster, as Nos. 137-171 and wide gauge cars as Nos. 172-211. Before the cars arrived, Mr. Johnson cancelled plans for wide gauge trackage and adopted standard gauge dimensions for Philadelphia and New York divisions. The transactions with St. Louis Car Company also included an order for a four wheel closed private car named "Electra".

The seventy-five St. Louis cars represented Lehigh Valley Traction Company's second acquisition of double truck cars. In August, 1900, the company had purchased six small type double truck cars from Third Avenue Railroad in New York City particularly for Allentown-Slatington service. The company identified the six cars as Nos. 129-134.

The first contingent of St. Louis cars arrived in Allentown on railroad flat cars on May 29, 1901. Traction company maintenance crews unloaded all cars at Riverside Yard located near Front and Linden streets and immediately placed them in storage under cover at carbarns in Hecktown, Butztown, Rittersville, and South Allentown and in open air storage in a long siding near Fullerton along the eastern Allentown-Catasauqua route. Mr. Johnson purposely withheld the cars from service until inauguration of interurban service over Philadelphia and New York divisions.

Albert L. Johnson's premature death on July 2, 1901, presaged the electric railway empire's ultimate collapse. Mr. Robert E. Wright, the capable Allentown attorney who succeeded Mr. Johnson as president, immediately investigated the company's financial status. After his study had been concluded he cancelled the Philadelphia-New York division, approved completion of the Allentown-Philadelphia route, and left undisturbed the leases with other companies in the Lehigh River valley. During March, 1902, St. Louis cars entered city and suburban service at the same time Philadelphia and Lehigh Valley Traction Company, the corporate title of the Allentown-Philadelphia route, inaugurated interurban service between Allentown and Quakertown.

Cancellation of more than one-half of Mr. Johnson's proposed interurban network provided more high speed St. Louis cars than could be economically assigned to existing routes. Consequently, brokers' advertisements in sundry 1902 issues of electric railway periodicals offered excess St. Louis cars for sale. Lehigh Valley Traction Company eventually sold twenty-nine cars as the result of these advertisements: eight wide gauge type cars to Fonda, Johnstown and Gloversville Railroad Company, New York; one wide gauge car to Citizens Electric and Gas Company, Iowa; two wide gauge cars to Danville

Lehigh Valley Traction Company car No. 128 stands on East Third Street, Bethlehem, circa 1905.
**(Nos. 125-128, Stephenson, 1900)**

Lehigh Valley Traction Company's car No. 133, bound for Allentown, stands in Northampton (Siegfrieds) at the end of the Allentown-Catasauqua-Northampton route, circa 1905.
**(Nos. 129-134, St. Louis, 1898, for Third Avenue Railroad, New York City; to LVT, 1900)**

Street Railway and Light Company, Illinois; and eight standard and ten wide gauge cars to Oakland Transit Consolidated, California. The traction company also transferred four wide gauge cars to Trenton, Lawrenceville and Princeton Railroad Company in New Jersey, the only portion of the proposed Philadelphia-New York route which ever operated. The transactions eliminated St. Louis cars Nos. 187-211 from the roster plus several of the standard gauge type. Meanwhile, as the sales continued, the traction company reconditioned the original eleven eight bench summer cars with which Allentown and Bethlehem Rapid Transit Company had inaugurated electric railway service in 1891 and renumbered them oddly Nos. 213-233.

Lehigh Valley Traction Company's financial status recorded no improvement during the second year following Albert L. Johnson's death. In lieu of cash rental due Easton Consolidated Electric Company on April 1, 1903, Lehigh Valley Traction Company temporarily postponed loss of lease by transferring four St. Louis cars to Easton Transit Company's ownership. On May 1, 1903, the traction company paid interest due Bethlehem and Nazareth Street Railway but defaulted payment due Philadelphia and Lehigh Valley Traction Company bonds. Consequently, on May 3, 1903, the Albert L. Johnson Estate applied for receivers in the United States District Court in Philadelphia. The court immediately appointed a receivership committee composed of business men and financiers who resided in the Allentown and Philadelphia areas.

Lehigh Valley Traction Company's inability to finance new track construction to cement plants located northward from Allentown brought aid from the cement industry itself. Several cement producers together organized, financed and constructed Whitehall Street Railway Company between Lehigh Valley

Traction Company's Egypt terminus and Levans village located southward from Schnecksville along the Allentown-Slatington route. Lehigh Valley Traction Company, contracted as operators, inaugurated service on July 24, 1903.

The traction company lost control of two leased companies through default of rental payment on March 1, 1904. Easton Consolidated Electric Company regained control of its properties and rolling stock on May 2, 1904, and Bethlehem Construction Company regained Slate Belt Electric Railway Company and two small double truck cars on May 4, 1904. Nazareth-Bangor and Easton-Bethlehem operations of the traction company ended with termination of leases. At the request of the reorganization committee, Mr. Charles Dupont, general manager of St. Louis electric railways, personally studied Lehigh Valley Traction Company's problems. His recommendations, issued May 7, 1904, suggested the expenditure of $1,800,000 to recondition track and right of way; construct a modern generating, transmission, and conversion power system; and acquire new lighter weight double truck cars.

Lehigh Valley Traction Company's financial situation reached the inevitable climax in 1905 when the receivership committee failed to persuade bond holders to trade an equal amount of first mortgage bonds for 60% second mortgage bond and 40% preferred stock. Most bond holders favored a public sale of properties. On May 6, 1905, Guarantee Trust Company of New York City predicted that a public sale would be conducted if the traction company defaulted its two million dollar payment of maturing bond coupons. The traction company's inability to meet this obligation had been a foregone conclusion.

## LEHIGH VALLEY TRANSIT COMPANY
## FORMED

William F. Harrity, representing most

Lehigh Valley Traction Company car No. 131 stands on Main Street, Hellertown, near terminus of Bethlehem-Hellertown route, circa 1905.

Lehigh Valley Transit Company summer car No. 39 stands at terminus of Allentown-Slatington route in Slatington prepared for trip to Slatedale via the branch route, 1907.
(No. 39, Kuhlman, 1906)

reorganization committee members, attended public sales conducted on the Lehigh County courthouse steps on June 13, 1905, and successfully bid one million dollars for Philadelphia and Lehigh Valley Traction Company (trackage only) and on June 20, 1905, successfully bid two hundred and seventy-five thousand dollars for Allentown and Slatington Street Railway Company (trackage only) and two million dollars for Lehigh Valley Traction Company (trackage and rolling stock) and Coplay, Egypt, and Ironton Street Railway Company (trackage only). Rolling stock acquired in the transaction included approximately one hundred and fifty cars of various types.

New ownership immediately produced a new organization. The owners merged all former Johnson street railway properties located in eastern Pennsylvania on July 20, 1905, and formed Lehigh Valley Transit Company. Five days later Harry C. Trexler, Edward M. Young, newly elected president and vice-president respectively, together with George O. Albright, Tom L. Johnson, William F. Harrity, George H. Frazier, Edward B. Smith, Arthur E. Newbold, and David Young formed the board of directors. Effective July 26, 1905, and continuing until the United States District Court in Philadelphia approved both sale and reorganization and Commonwealth of Pennsylvania approved a new charter, the properties operated as Lehigh Valley Passenger Railway, Allentown and Slatington Passenger Railway, and Philadelphia and Lehigh Valley Passenger Railway. One single truck car temporarily carried a Lehigh Valley Passenger Railway designation for legality purposes.

Lehigh County's Recorder of Deeds received Lehigh Valley Transit Company's charter, dated November 3, 1905, from Commonwealth of Pennsylvania on November 16, 1905. Meanwhile, the new owners commenced improvements: approved construction of a large modern powerhouse equipped with 25 cycle AC turbo-generators and a 13,200 volt three phase power distribution system with substations; ordered ninety-six pound rail, Trilby pattern, from Loraine Steel Works; ordered ten closed and ten semi-convertible medium weight double truck cars from The J. G. Brill Company in Philadelphia, Pennsylvania; and approved purchase of land at Fourteenth and Gordon streets in northwest Allentown for erection of new shops, a carbarn, and on office building. Lehigh Valley Transit Company divided its operations into Allentown and Philadelphia divisions and established South Allentown Carbarn as center of the former and Souderton Carbarn as center of the latter. Each division maintained a seniority run-selection list for both motormen and conductors.

Ten double truck standard medium weight semi-convertible cars Nos. 187-196, built by Kuhlman Car Company, and ten similar closed cars Nos. 197-206, built by American Car Company, arrived in Allentown between November 22, and December 12, 1905, and replaced single truck cars assigned to Allentown-Egypt and Allentown-Freemansburg routes and shared services with St. Louis cars on Allentown-Emaus-Macungie and Allentown-Bethlehem-Hellertown routes. Although the cars had been purchased to replace St. Louis cars on all routes except Philadelphia Division, increased patronage required retention of St. Louis cars.

During 1906 the improvement program continued: on May 8, twenty ten-bench single truck summer cars numbered below one hundred, the second new car purchase authorized by the new organization, replaced older similar cars which had been either sold or scrapped; during summer months the line department crews completed the installation of poles for high tension power lines along Slatington and Naz-

Car No. 303 stands before Bethlehem Fairgrounds at intersection of Elizabeth Avenue, Linden Street, and Easton Avenue, circa, 1909. (Nos. 301-304, Brill, 1908)

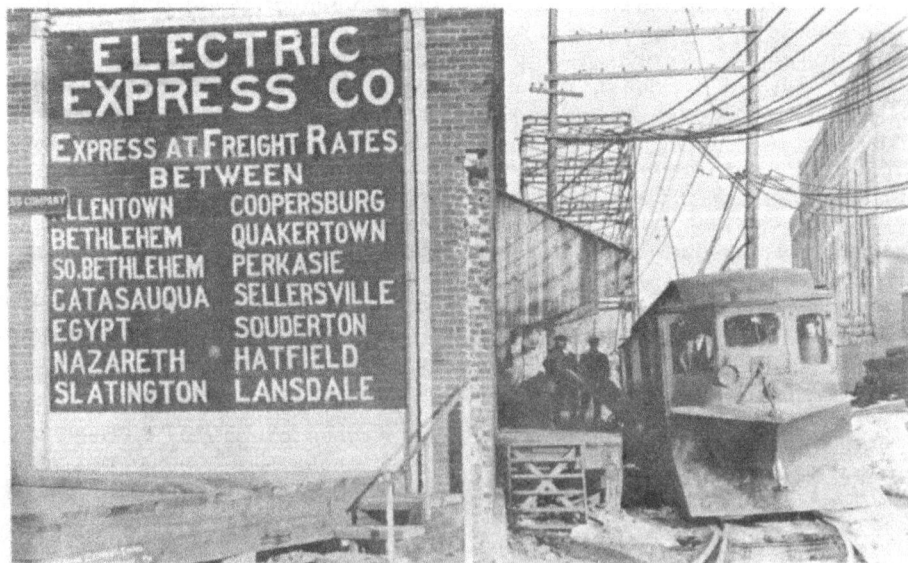

ELECTRIC EXPRESS CO.

EXPRESS AT FREIGHT RATES BETWEEN

| | |
|---|---|
| LLENTOWN | COOPERSBURG |
| BETHLEHEM | QUAKERTOWN |
| SO. BETHLEHEM | PERKASIE |
| CATASAUQUA | SELLERSVILLE |
| EGYPT | SOUDERTON |
| NAZARETH | HATFIELD |
| SLATINGTON | LANSDALE |

Freight car No. C2, equipped with plow for snow duty, stands at Allentown freight house located on North Front Street near Linden Street, circa 1910. (Nos. C2 and C3, Brill, 1909)

areth routes; and the company announced the forthcoming construction of new substations at Slatington and Siegersville along the Slatington route, Hecktown along the Nazareth route, Catasauqua along the Northampton-Siegfried route, and in Bethlehem.

Lehigh Valley Transit Company on March 9, 1907, moved passenger and most work equipment into the new fifty-car capacity 14th Street Carbarn. As the result of this move the surrounding locality eventually included paint, carpenter, machine, and electric shops; for several years, the line department; a car storage yard; dispatcher's headquarters; and main office. South Allentown Carbarn served as a work equipment center briefly prior to its sale to a private manufacturer. During April, 1907, two new single truck closed cars Nos. 102 and 105 arrived to replace older similar cars assigned to Allentown and Bethlehem city local service.

Acquisition of new cars between 1905 and 1907 permitted the scrapping of twenty-five older single truck open and twenty single truck closed cars. Maintenance crews dismantled and burned the wooden cars in the derail spur of Philadelphia Division's main line located midway on the northern slope of Lehigh, or South, Mountain.

Mr. R. P. Stevens, a University of Maine graduate who had also completed post-graduate courses at Massachusetts Institute of Technology, accepted Lehigh Valley Transit Company's presidency on July 7, 1907. Mr. Stevens had served Auburn and Syracuse Railway Company in New York as general manager at the time of his election. The new president assumed executive duties on August 15, 1907, and during his six-year administration directed Lehigh Valley Transit Company's rise from a secondary position to one of the outstanding street railway properties located in eastern United States.

Monthly executive meetings produced directives for physical improvements as well as announcements of projects completed. Publicity releases announced during October, 1907, included the completion of a huge power plant equipped with 500, 1000, and 2500 horsepower turbines; commencement of the telephone system's installation along Slatington route and Philadelphia Division; adoption of chrome green, red, black and gold trim paint scheme in place of Broadway yellow, tan, cream, silver and black colors which had identified equipment since 1895; and identification of rolling stock with a LVT scroll monogram. After the telephone system had been installed and phones had been placed at convenient locations, dispatchers located in the main office directed movements over Allentown Division's routes.

Expansion of Bethlehem Steel Company's Bethlehem Plant in 1906 required trackage revision along the South Bethlehem-Hellertown route. The transit company abandoned track along Second Street eastward from New Street to a point near Northampton Heights, except a short spur which served the South Bethlehem carbarn and freight house, and built new track along Third Street and Daly Avenue. Originally, trackage had followed Second Street to Northampton Heights although a short circumvention of the steel plant had required construction of track along Third Street for two city blocks. Completion of Northampton Heights Bridge over Philadelphia and Reading Railway Company in 1908 eliminated a physical crossing of the railroad spur which led into the steel plant and placed track on an overhead ramp, which extended from Daly Avenue onto the bridge, and formed a connection with original trackage located on Fourth Street.

In January, 1908, the transit company acquired four new small single truck closed cars Nos. 126-129 for

Car No. 197, operating Allentown-Emaus-Macungie service, stands at terminus of trackage in Macungie prepared for return trip to Allentown, circa 1909.
(Nos. 197-206, American, 1905)

ɔnvertible type fitted for summer operations, stands at 17th and Hamilton Streets, Allentown, prepared for Allentown-Bethlehem trip, circa 1911.
(Nos. 600-609, Brill, 1910)

replacement of larger single truck cars which had been scrapped. The cars represented the first new cars to be equipped with illuminated roller destination signs and an electric heating system. In order to retain consecutive numbering, the company renumbered closed double truck Third Avenue-type car No. 129 to No. 135. The two double truck cars originally numbered 135 and 136 had been returned to Slate Belt Electric Railway Company with termination of the lease in 1904.

Signing of the trolley freight law by Pennsylvania's governor on April 25, 1907, found most companies unprepared to immediately offer the new service. Lehigh Valley Transit Company introduced freight service between Allentown and Bethlehem in 1908 with converted single truck passenger car No. 98 and Philadelphia Division freight service with a small single truck box-type car built in 14th Street Shop and identified as No. B1. Later, the company revised a double truck snow plow for freight service. Freight service eventually expanded over all routes to the extent that by World War I the roster listed thirteen various type double truck freight cars identified as C Series. Allentown Division established freight houses in Allentown, South Behtlehem, and Slatington, but the traditional country general store standing near the right of way usually served as both shipping and receiving points along rural and suburban routes.

After the four double truck deck roof open passenger cars Nos. 301-304, purchased in spring, 1908, failed to produce anticipated results in Philadelphia Division's Delaware Water Gap excursion service between Chestnut Hill and Portland, the transit company assigned the cars to Allentown Division for local summer service assignments in Allentown and Bethlehem. The cars, identified as 301 Series and the first new cars painted green, ended the

consecutive numbering policy and established the series system of identification.

Four new single truck closed cars identified as Nos. 406-409 arrived in August, 1909, from The J.G. Brill Company for use in local service in Allentown and Bethlehem business districts. These four cars plus the six single truck cars purchased previously and renumbered Nos. 400-405, established the 400 Series group. Later, the transit company revamped Albert E. Johnson's private car named "Electra" as passenger car No. 410. The car, originally equipped with desk, chairs, and sofa, had served variously as an inspection, charter, and pay car after Mr. Johnson's death.

Throughout its entire railway history Lehigh Valley Transit Company's roster listed a variety of single and double truck utility and non-revenue equipment which either had been built in company shops, purchased, or converted from passenger cars. Types included snow sweeper, snow plough, flat trailer, line, grease, lamp, rail bond, rail bond tester, sand, derrick, scarifier, and stone cars. The stone car, between assignments, usually stood under the small crusher which the transit company maintained in East Allentown until the late 1920's. The company, with few exceptions, identified utility and non-revenue cars in A, B, C, D, F, R, S, T, and 500 Series groups.

Allentown's population growth during the first decade of the Twentieth Century required the expansion of electric railway service. On September 21, 1909, track crews completed trackage which extended from North Sixth and Gordon streets intersection via Gordon, Jordan, and Tilghman streets to a connection with the eastern Allentown-Fullerton route at Ridge Avenue. At the same time, by laying track on Jordan and Washington streets from North Jordan and Tilghman streets intersec-

Bethlehem-bound freight car No. B1 stands on Bethlehem-Nazareth route southward from Hecktown, circa 1913.
(No. B1, LVT, 1908)

Line car No. 503 stands on Broad Street westward from New Street in Bethlehem, circa 1916.
(Nos. 501-504, LVT, 1905)

tion to a connection with the Allentown-Northampton route at North Fourth and Washington streets intersection the company established a route identified later as Seventh Street loop. Another route which served Allentown's north end residents opened on October 9, 1909, from a connection with trackage at Tenth and Hamilton streets intersection along North Tenth, Allen, North Ninth, and Washington streets to a connection with existing trackage at North Seventh and Washington streets intersection. Later, by rerouting schedules this trackage received the identification as Tenth Street loop.

Circa 1910 Lehigh Valley Transit Company's 14th Street Shop revised St. Louis car No. 176 as a combination baggage and passenger car. Although No. 176 usually hauled milk, mail, and newspapers over Philadelpia Division it also appeared frequently in funeral service over other routes. The wide doorway permitted convenient loading of the coffin. Other type cars as well as other St. Louis cars received funeral assignments along most rural routes as well as the hauling of mail. During the same year the transit company built a small carbarn in Slatington to house and service cars which maintained Slatington-Slatedale schedules and which operated Slatington-Allentown daily schedules commencing in Slatington.

## PAY AS YOU ENTER SERVICE ESTABLISHED

The quest for economical and convenient service dictated the purchase of more new cars beginning in 1910. Ten double truck semi-lightweight deck roof convertible pay-within Brill cars Nos. 600-609, patterned after Third Avenue Railroad Company's (New York) convertible cars with variations, introduced on July 22, 1910; ten similar but arch roof convertible pay-as-you-enter type cars Nos. 610-619,

equipped with lifeguards instead of Providence fenders, effective June 16, 1911; and four slightly heavier but similar cars Nos. 620-623, ordered February 14, 1912, between 1910 and 1912 replaced St. Louis cars in various Allentown, Bethlehem, South Bethlehem, and Hellertown services. Interchangeable window panels and screens adapted all twenty-four cars to both winter and summer use. The transit company inaugurated pay-as-you-enter fare collection system on December 18, 1911, on local routes in Allentown and Bethlehem after revising cars Nos. 600-609. Previously, passengers entered the rear door, occupied a seat, paid their fare after seated, and disembarked via the front door. Cars Nos. 610-619 were the first new cars acquired by the company which were equipped with mechanical folding doors and steps.

Lehigh Valley Transit Company's acquisition of Montgomery Traction Company's wide gauge route between Lansdale and Norristown on October 25, 1911, provided right of way privileges for construction of the revised Liberty Bell Route. Two double truck and two single truck closed railroad roof type cars accompanied the transaction. Allentown Division reduced the cars' truck gauge, applied the standard paint scheme, and assigned Nos. 207 and 208 to the double truck cars and Nos. 411 and 412 to the single truck cars. The former received assignments normally assigned to 187 Series cars and the latter to those operated by 400 Series cars.

Circa 1912 the transit company converted Allentown Division's signal system from the conventional manual type to the more efficient and modern Nachod automatic trolley pole contact system. Electric and line department crews initially installed the new system along trackage located on Lehigh River Bridge and St. John Street viaduct in Allentown, on New Street Bridge in

23

Fairgrounds-bound car No. 197 accommodates passengers at 6th and Hamilton Streets intersection before American Hotel in Allentown, September, 1920.

Snow plow No. 519 de-railed by deep snow along Bethlehem-Nazareth route near Macada, circa 1920.
(Nos. 519, 520, and ETCo No. 10, LVT, 1919)

24

Bethlehem, and along Allentown-Bethlehem pike in West Bethlehem. By 1916 the entire Allentown Division had been converted to the automatic system.

Allentown Division assigned St. Louis cars Nos. 144 and 150, one as an alternate car, to "Easton Limited" service inaugurated jointly with Easton Transit Company between Allentown and Easton via Bethlehem effective March 17, 1913. Each day Lehigh Valley Transit Company supplied one car and Easton Transit Company one lighter weight double truck 205 Series car. Lehigh Valley Transit Company's crews manned cars between Allentown and Bethlehem and Easton Transit Company's crews between Bethlehem and Easton. At the meeting point in Bethlehem passengers remained in their respective cars but both crews transferred from one car to another. St. Louis cars operated the schedules until Easton Transit Company purchased, at intervals beginning in 1914, ten large arch roof steel double truck 214 Series Brill cars and assumed complete responsibility for the limited operation. A one way trip between both cities consumed one hour.

During summer, 1913, the transit company created loop trackage in Bethlehem and South Bethlehem by constructing trackage eastward along Broad Street from Linden Street to Newton Avenue (Stefko Boulevard) and southward along Newton Avenue and across newly constructed Minsi Trail Bridge to a wye connection with the Bethlehem-Hellertown route at Daly Avenue in South Bethlehem. The trackage permitted the establishment of more flexible service for Bethlehem Steel Company's Bethlehem Plant. In autumn, 1913, Lehigh Valley Transit Company and Slate Belt Electric Railway Company entered into a freight transfer arrangement which benefited merchants and farmers between Allentown and Bangor. In Fairground Siding, Nazareth, crews transferred freight from one company's car to the other for conveyance to destination. Also, in 1913, Lehigh Valley Transit Company reduced the St. Louis car roster with the sale of car No. 142 to Pottsville Union Traction Company, Pottsville, Pennsylvania.

Easton Transit Company and associated organizations entered Lehigh Valley Transit Company's sphere of influence effective July, 1913, by the latter's purchase of controlling shares of Easton Consolidated Electric Company's stock. At the same time, with R. P. Stevens' resignation as president, Lehigh Valley Transit Company's board of directors elected H. R. Fehr, president of Easton Transit Company, as Mr. Stevens' successor. Mr. Fehr served both companies during his tenure.

Effective November 13, 1913, the opening of Eighth Street Bridge across Lehigh Creek valley which separated South Allentown from Allentown's business district altered all street railway routes which entered Allentown from southerly directions. The 1,950 foot compound arch reinforced concrete structure, built by a subsidiary organization of the transit company, stood one hunred and thirty-eight feet above Lehigh Creek's bed at the highest point and represented the largest structure of its type in the world. In addition, new double track construction extended westward along St. John Street from South Sixth Street to South Eighth Street and northward along South Eighth Street across the bridge and formed wye connections with existing trackage on Hamilton Street. Eighth and Hamilton streets intersection immediately replaced Sixth and Hamilton streets as the transit company's center in Allentown's business district. Philadelphia Division's limited and local service terminated and commenced schedules at that point, but most of Allentown Division's suburban, city, and rural routes merely served the intersection as part of regular service.

25

St. Louis car No. 153, assigned to snow duty, ascends Main Street hill in Slatington enroute to Allentown, circa 1920.
(Nos. 137-186, St. Louis, 1901)

No. 404 represents the condition of car bodies at the commencement of the 1920-1923 rebuilding program.
(Nos. 402-405, Brill, 1908)

Lehigh Valley Transit Company and predecessors maintained various car-barns for Allentown Division's use: Madison Street, Allentown, 1889-1939; Ritterville, 1892-1914; South Allentown, 1893-1909; Hecktown, 1899-1932; South Bethlehem, 1899-1918; 14th Street, Allentown, 1907-1939; and Slatington, 1910-1931. On April 11, 1914, a dismantling crew removed the small Rittersville Carbarn's walls, roof, and foundation but left the tracks intact for yard storage purposes, and on May 18, 1914, the transit company opened modern spacious Fairview Carbarn in South Allentown. Trackage reached Fairview Carbarn via St. John and Lehigh streets from track located at South Eighth and St. John streets intersection. Allentown Division routes, with only a few exceptions, operated from the new structure. The modern building also provided facilities for Allentown Division's dispatching headquarters. Carpenter, paint, mechanical, line, and electrical departments remained near 14th and Gordon streets after opening of Fairview Carbarn and the track and switch department continued operations from the original location in Riverside Yard.

Completion of single track construction on Union Street between Lehigh Street and north entrance of Eighth Street Bridge on October 19, 1914, established trackage identified thereafter as Union Street loop. The route provided an outlet which eliminated many movements which ordinarily operated back to Fairview Carbarn through traffic-congested Eighth and Hamilton streets intersection and also provided uninvolved reversal facilities for Philadelphia Division's local cars.

Between 1914 and 1916 the transit company modernized all passenger cars: permanent semi-flush incandescent headlights installed on the dash beneath front and rear center windows replaced the portable carbon arc plug-in type; permanent wooden slat H-B lifeguards

fastened beneath both platforms replaced the cumbersome Providence fender; and small wire screen guards were removed from closed cars' side windows. The program also included the conversion of open cars Nos. 301-304 to a convertible type similar to 600 series cars. Primarily as a protective measure, 14th Street Shop between 1917 and 1923 covered the exposed bumper lip of St. Louis, convertible, Third Avenue, and 400 Series cars with steel sheets but allowed a niche for the draw bar jaw. In addition to the protective value against the elements, steel sheets eliminated the common, but dangerous, practice of having as many as six passengers standing on the rear bumper of crowded cars.

Lehigh Power Securities Corporation, a National Power and Light Company subsidiary, acquired control of Lehigh Valley Transit Company on July 19, 1917, and procured Electric Bond and Share Company's managerial service. The transaction transferred the transit company's financial influence from Philadelphia to New York. As immediate visual evidence of new ownership, the managers changed the paint scheme from chrome green, gold, yellow, and black colors to bright red, brown stain, gold, sand, and black colors. Many months passed before all cars had been repainted. Difficulty in obtaining red pigment from Tuscany during World War I slowed adoption of the new paint scheme temporarily and caused repainting of some cars in various shades of green.

## CENTER ENTRANCE CARS PURCHASED

Plant expansion and increased production established by Lehigh Valley area's industries during World War I required additional street railway equipment to transport workers between homes and factories. Through finances granted by wartime federal agencies the transit company ordered

27

Car No. 402 shows the results of the 1920-1923 modernization program.

Car No. 208, ex-Montgomery Traction Company's car No. 2, reveals the condition of car bodies prior to the 1920-1923 modernization program. (MTC Nos. 1 and 2, Stephenson, 1902; LVT Nos. 207 and 208, 1912)

twenty-four medium weight double truck steel closed center entrance multiple unit 900 Series cars from The J. G. Brill Company on June 1, 1917, and fifteen similar type in 1919. Effective March, 1918, the 900 Series cars replaced St. Louis cars in Allentown-Catasauqua-Northampton service, various type cars in Allentown-Bethlehem South Bethlehem service, and sundry local runs which operated in Allentown. However, although fully equipped, the 900 Series cars never operated as trains in revenue service. During February, 1918, the transit company also purchased eight ten-bench summer car bodies from Philadelphia Rapid Transit Company to replaced eight smaller open cars which had been scrapped.

During World War I Allentown Division completed a project which proved to be its last major track construction. The new route extended northeastward from a point designated as Minsi Trail Junction, located at Broad Street and Newton Avenue (Stefko Boulevard) in Bethlehem, through Pembroke to a wye connection with the Bethlehem-Easton route at Browns Siding located westward from Butztown. A federal government housing project constructed near Pembroke and Bethlehem Steel Company's Bethlehem Plant, engaged in production of war materials, dictated construction of new trackage. Before United States entry into World War I the transit company installed a "grand union" trackage crossover (two paralleling tracks leading in all three directions from each approach) at Broad and New streets intersection in Bethlehem's business district. The arrangement, the only one of its type ever constructed by Lehigh Valley Transit Company, also represented one of the few ever installed in the United States.

Between 1913 and 1920 the transit company operated over the maximum total of track mileage which the system ever achieved. Including all trackage

of all three divisions which had been either built or leased, Lehigh Valley Transit Company's operations extended one hundred and ninety-six route miles. Second track, sidings, and connections accounted for twenty-eight additional miles of trackage.

Between 1920 and 1923 the transit company conducted a major rolling stock rehabilitation program which modernized, revised, and painted most city and suburban type cars. The installation of mechanical doors and steps represented the prime innovation. As part of improved operations the transit company also discontinued the use of summer cars in the early 1920's. Thereafter, the open cars slowly deteriorated in Fairview Carbarn yard and in 13th and Gordon streets storage yard. By 1929 all open cars had been scrapped. Circa 1919 the 14th Street Shop restored St. Louis combine car No. 176 to its original all-coach structure.

Lehigh Valley Transit Company, the majority stock holder, leased Easton Transit Company and associated organizations for ninety-nine years effective March 1, 1922, and designated the properties as Easton Division. Eventually, the familiar LVT scroll monogram replaced the ETCo identification on ninety-eight cars involved in the transation. Thereafter, whenever the need arose, Allentown Division transferred cars to Easton Division's roster.

In 1923 the transit company built another route between South Eighth and St. John streets intersection and Fairview Carbarn in Allentown in order to handle more efficiently movements to- and from the carbarn. The new track followed St. John, South Lumber, and West Cumberland streets to a connection with original trackage on Lehigh Street near the carbarn's entrance. As the result of this construction, the original route via Lehigh Street served westbound and the new route served eastbound movements. In 1934 a highway paving project caused abandon-

Center entrance car No. 900 posed for equipment photograph by the transit company at 14th Street Carbarn, Allentown, circa 1920. (Nos. 900-923, Brill, 1918)

Rebuilt car No. 906 and wheel car No. B1 stand before 14th Street Carbarn, Allentown, circa 1927. The structure shows initial conversion proceedings to an autobus garage.

ment of most of the Lehigh Street route and adaptation of the West Cumberland Street route by new construction and installation of switches to both directional movements.

After construction of Bethlehem's hill-to-hill bridge across Lehigh River in 1924, although track had been installed, Lehigh Valley Transit Company established autobus service over the main route with new vehicles rather than connect trackage with existing railway routes. In 1926 the transit company expanded its autobus roster with purchase of additional units to serve the College Heights community which had developed alongside Allentown's northwest boundary. The transit company's officials established 14th Street Carbarn as the center of autobus operations and provided additional storage space for vehicles by removing tracks from the yard which paralleled the south side of the carbarn and by constructing a garage on the site. In addition, autobus operations had been chartered as Lehigh Valley Transportation Company effective March 6, 1925.

Competition from privately owned automobiles prompted the transit company to modernize interiors of city-suburban cars. During late April, 1926, 14th Street Shop released center entrance car No. 902 as the first car to be refurbished: leather upholstered cushion type seats replaced the rattan type; electric seat heaters replaced the coal heater and ducts; spaced dome lights replaced the continuous rack of exposed lamps; a brown fibre board replaced glass in the upper window sash and thereby eliminated Pantasote shades; and an electric button fare register system with a pipe arrangement replaced rods and straps. Advertisements placed in local newspapers and cards inserted in advertising racks located inside all street railway cars suggested to local citizens that patronage of street railway service eliminated annoying parking and traffic worries

which accompanied operation of privately owned automobiles. Also, the company at this time removed all single truck closed passenger cars from revenue service.

Revitalization of freight service also received the company's attention. In May, 1927, the transit company inaugurated a store door pick-up and delivery service over all routes with a fleet of motor trucks which supplemented, and in some instances replaced, electric freight car service as a means to compete with rival motor truck companies. Eleven years later, in 1938, after successfully establishing a convenient service, the transit company sold its motor truck franchise to a competitor and contracted with the purchaser to haul its freight in electric cars directly between Allentown, Easton, and Philadelphia.

Attempts by transit companies in the United States to compete effectively with privately owned automobiles failed and forced the companies to pursue a policy of curtailment. Lehigh Valley Transit Company, following the national trend, replaced two man crews with a one man operation over city routes in 1927, and 14th Street Shop quickly adapted cars for the new arrangement. End entrance cars required only the installation of an electric fare recording system at control positions but center entrance 900 Series cars required costly structural revisions. Periodically, between 1927 and 1939 the mechanical department converted thirty-two of thirty-nine 900 Series center entrance cars into a straight side end entrance type which included interior furnishings and operating equipment similar to that installed on car No. 902 in 1926. The other 900 Series cars received a less extensive adjustment which included the bolting shut of center doors and widening right front and left rear doors. Shortly after one man service commenced the company introduced a modified paint

Car No. 612, a convertible type, moves westward along Hamilton Street towards 17th Street enroute to Allentown's 19th Street Section, circa 1930.
(Nos. 610-619, Brill, 1911)

Car No. 940, maintaining the Fairview Loop schedule in Allentown, stands on South 8th Street southward from Walnut Street, circa 1932.
(No. 940, experimental car, LVT, 1930, built over frame of No. 206)

scheme: dark red varnished body; brown stained window sashes and doors; silver striping, medium size numbers, monograms, roof, poles, bumper, and headlights; and black undercarriage replaced the bright red, gold, sand, and black combination introduced in 1917. At this time the company installed one of two types of shop-made marker lights on all city-suburban cars assigned to all divisions as a safety measure.

A circuit breaker fire severely damaged lightweight double truck car No. 206 on January 25, 1929, during Richlandtown-Quakertown local schedules of the Philadelphia Division and provided a damaged car for a modernization experiment conducted by the superintendent of equipment. The 14th Street Shop released the car, identified as No. 940, in 1930. Main features included a wide sloping windshield; built-in marker lights; tapered body ends; left hand modern control system; inward folding doors and outward folding step; trucks equipped with four motors and a short axle which extended from each motor to each wheel; and a safety control system which opened doors simultaneously with emergency application of the air brakes. Briefly, the car received a regular assignment to Seventh Street loop service in Allentown but subsequently acquired a spare car status for all city-suburban routes.

Despite adverse financial conditions which followed the stock market failure in 1929 and increasing competition from automobiles, the transit company purchased ten modern Brill one man city-suburban cars identified as 950 Series in autumn, 1930, and withdrew two man center entrance 900 Series cars from Allentown-Bethlehem and Hellertown services. New features, some of which reflected No. 940's designs, included inward folding doors but no outward step; interior stairway; narrow treadle rear door (never used) opposite wide entrance; automatic left

side control system with emergency braking features; built-in marker lights; and wide windshield with a visor. One of the new cars stood on exhibition on temporary track placed directly southward from the monument in Center Square, Allentown, between October 12, and 18, inclusive. People who inspected the car received, from a uniformed crew member, an invitation card which allowed one free ride.

## TRACK MILEAGE SHRINKS

While street railway systems in the United States struggled with competitors the depression added more financial woes. Many railway systems failed to survive these staggering burdens, but Lehigh Valley Transit Company, by virtue of well constructed trackage and well maintained cars retained most city-suburban routes but abandoned almost all of the rural routes. Between 1928 and 1932 Allentown Division abandoned Tilghman Street local route, Jordan Street to Ridge Avenue, Allentown, 1928; Emaus-Macungie, May 31, 1929; Slatington-Slatedale, June, 1929; Egypt-Levans (Whitehall Street Railway Company), January 31, 1931; Catasauqua-Egypt via Coplay, June 30, 1931; Greenawalds-Slatington, July 31, 1931; Mountainville-Emaus, October 31, 1931; Bethlehem - Nazareth, February 29, 1932; and Elizabeth Avenue, Main and Church streets local service, Bethlehem, 1932. Autobus service in most, but not all, cases replaced discontinued railway operations. Construction of Tilghman Street Bridge across Lehigh River in 1927-1928 caused relocation of Allentown-Fullerton route trackage along Ridge Avenue between Allen and Tilghman streets and along Tilghman Street from Ridge Avenue to Front Street with new trackage construction along Front Street between Tilghman and Allen streets and along Allen Street between Front Street and Ridge Avenue. Trackage adjustments usually caused the establishment of new routes

33

Howard P. Sell Collection

Car No. 58 of Public Service of Wisconsin, Green Bay, being unloaded at Riverside Yard, Allentown, to commence the 1938-1940 modernization program, July 22, 1938.
**(PSW Nos. 57 and 58, American, 1926; LVT Nos. 401 and 400, 1938)**

Rev. Samuel P. Worthington

Car No. 400, ex-Public Service of Wisconsin Company No. 58 and car No. 1100, ex-Dayton and Troy Electric Railway Company No. 201, stand on public exhibition on the south side of Center Square, Allentown, February 5, 1939.

and schedules . At the end of 1932 the transit company and its subsidiaries operated one hundred and fifty-five miles of street railway service and one hundred and forty-four miles of autobus routes.

Prior to the abandonment program Allentown Division's operating schedules, in relation to time consumed between Allentown and outlying termini, had been established approximately as follows: Slatington, one hour; Northampton via Fullerton and Catasauqua, forty-five minutes; Nazareth via Bethlehem, one hour; Macungie via Emmaus (Emaus), one hour; Bethlehem, one-half hour; and Egypt via Fullerton, Catasauqua, and Coplay, one hour. Various local schedules operating within Allentown and Bethlehem confines offered service which ranged from fifteen minutes to one-half hour between terminal points.

Abandonment of routes produced an excess amount of rolling stock, and deteriorating cars eventually clogged Fairview Yard trackage. Between 1920 and 1935, with most activity recorded during 1934 and 1935, the transit company eliminated eighty-six passenger and ten utility cars from the roster. In 1935, while Fairview Carbarn's maintenance crews scrapped obsolete cars, the transit company acquired five short double truck lightweight steel-constructed cars from Williamsport Railway Company, Williamsport, Pennsylvania, for use in Fairview-Gordon streets and 10th Street loop local service in Allentown. The transit company identified the cars as Nos. 960-964 and thereby established the 960 Series.

After the scrap program had been completed, Lehigh Valley Transit Company assigned less power consuming 900, 950, and 960 Series cars to regular service over the remaining routes of Allentown Division. Car No. 940; many, but not all, 137 Series St. Louis cars; 301 Series; and 600 Series cars which

had survived the scrap program received spare and rush hour assignments. Heavy snow storms which struck the Lehigh Valley area during winter, 1935-1936, incapacitated lighter lower cars to the extent that the transit company temporarily reactivated seven other St. Louis cars and almost as many 600 Series cars which had stood in storage for several years in Fairview Carbarn's yard.

Moderate financial recovery and increased production in the Lehigh Valley area's industries in late 1936 and early 1937 required additional equipment for regular service. The company quickly rehabilitated and repainted many of the stored cars. The same program changed the standard color scheme for all regular city and suburban cars from the red, silver, and black scheme to a red body; cream window sashes; silver roof and poles; gold striping, small numbers, and monograms; and black bumpers, headlights, and undercarriage. Before the new style had been selected the company applied experimental blue and silver, red and silver, orange and silver, gray and black, and sand and black color schemes to several 900 and 950 Series cars. During this period the transit company rehabilitated many miles of track with particular emphasis upon trackage which extended through the business districts of Allentown and Bethlehem.

## 1938-1940 MODERNIZATION PROGRAM

Engineers engaged by Electric Bond and Share Company in 1938 evaluated Lehigh Valley Transit Company's position as a street railway operator and recommended retention of Allentown and Bethlehem city trackage and rail routes to Greenawalds, Northampton, South Bethlehem, Bethlehem, Hellertown, and Easton; retention of the Liberty Bell Route; conversion of Easton Division's city routes to autobus service; reconditioning of the company's

35

Car No. 909, a center entrance car partially converted for one man service, stands on North 7th Street northward from Hamilton Street, Allentown, while maintaining the Allentown-Catasauqua-Northampton schedule, May 2, 1939.

Double truck snow sweeper No. 523 crosses 6th and St. John Streets intersection, Allentown, on February 13, 1940.
(No. 523, LVT, 1923; converted from passenger car No. 134)

36

newer cars; and acquisition of newer second-hand city-suburban type street railway cars to replace all older types. The transit company immediately commenced a modernization program the likes of which only a few street railway companies ever conducted in the United States. William B. McGorum, the newly elected vice president and general manager, directed the program which extended from late spring, 1938, until August, 1940.

Between 1936 and 1940 Allentown Division revised the rolling stock roster by scrapping fifty-three passenger and thirteen utility cars and rehabilitating fifty-eight passenger cars and thirty-one utility cars. In addition, through Utility Equipment Company, railway equipment brokers, the transit company acquired twenty-two second hand lightweight double truck city-suburban type cars from defunct companies scattered throughout United States: two, Public Service of Wisconsin, Green Bay; fourteen, Ohio Valley Electric Railway Company, Huntingdon, West Virginia; and six, Jamestown Street Railway Company, Jamestown, New York. The transaction also included twenty-three interurban type cars: four for Easton Division; and thirteen limited and six local types for Philadelphia Division. Fairview Carbarn and 14th Street Carbarn rehabilitated all cars and adapted them to Lehigh Valley Transit Company's mode of operation. The program reactivated the 400 Series classification formerly assigned to single truck city cars and added 1000 Series and 1100 Series for the newly acquired interurban cars.

Coincidental with the modernization program Lehigh Valley Transit Company adopted another paint scheme for Allentown Division's cars: mountain ash scarlet body, headlights, and bumpers; picador cream window sash and stripe on bumpers; small gold numbers but no monograms; and black undercarriage. Work and utility equipment re-

ceived a similar adornment.. After the cars had been reconditioned and painted, Allentown Division assigned 900 Series cars to Allentown-South Bethlehem-Bethlehem and Bethlehem-Hellertown routes; 950 Series cars to Allentown-Bethlehem service; 960 Series cars to 10th Street Loop and Fairview-Gordon Street routes in Allentown; and 410 Series cars, the former Ohio Valley Electric Railway Company cars, to the Allentown-Catasauqua-Northampton route. The 400 Series cars, former Public Service of Wisconsin, Green Bay, cars; 440 Series cars, former Jamestown Street Railway Company cars; and the transit company's 600 Series and 214 Series cars, the latter acquired from Easton Division after abandonment of city service, served as spare cars along with excess cars of other groups.

After the modernization program had been concluded the transit company moved all maintenance and mechanical facilities from and near 14th and Gordon streets to Fairview Carbarn and sold abandoned property to various independent buyers. Coincidental with the maneuver the line department, which had also been located near South Sixth and Union streets, joined the track and switch department at Riverside Yard.

Entry of United States into World War II and accompanying controls and regulations transferred mass transportation from privately owned highway vehicles to public transportation systems. Lehigh Valley Transit Company efficiently served the public during this period. Every day all available rolling stock moved workers between homes and factories at shift changes. The transit company supplemented its passenger car roster by returning deck roof utility cars Nos. 302 and 304, passenger cars converted to utility use in 1939, to passenger service in summer, 1942.

After hostilities had ended and government agencies had removed in-

Car No. 441, ex-Jamestown Street Railway Company No. 80, stands on yard trackage at Fairview Carbarn, Allentown, March 16, 1940. (JSR Nos. 79-83 and 85, St. Louis, 1918; LVT Nos. 440-445, 1939)

Allentown-bound No. 421, ex-Ohio Valley Electric Railway Co. car No. 237, enters Fullerton from West Catasauqua while maintaining the Allentown-Catasauqua-Northampton schedule, circa 1950. (OVER Nos. 225 and 227-239, Kuhlman, 1927; LVT Nos. 410-423, 1938-1939)

dustrial production controls, citizens returned to privately owned automobiles for their transportation needs. Once again Lehigh Valley Transit Company's patronage and revenues declined. Constant use of street cars in expanded services and lack of repair materials either in quantity or quality, all results of wartime regulations, caused abnormal wear on rolling stock and trackage between 1941 and 1945. Official surveys revealed that only another extensive modernization program could restore property and rolling stock to prewar standards. Instead, although a modest repair program had been underway, the transit company instituted a program which gradually substituted autobuses for electric railway cars. At the time of the decision the company maintained two hundred and twenty-seven route miles of autobus service and one hundred and eighteen route miles of electric railway service in its three operating divisions. Rolling stock included one hundred and fifty railway cars and one hundred and eleven autobuses.

Discontinuance of Easton Division's Easton - Bethlehem - Allentown limited service and abandonment of track between Minsi Trail Junction, Bethlehem, and Centre Square, Easton, in August, 1949, resulted in the transfer of four lightweight interurban passenger and five miscellaneous utility cars to Allentown Division's roster. Allentown Division retained the utility cars, scrapped passenger cars Nos. 1101 and 1103 and sold cars Nos. 1100 and 1102 to Milwaukee and Speedrail Company, Kenosha, Wisconsin. Allentown Division, in another move toward motorized operations, converted the heavily patronized Tenth Street loop service from street railway car to autobus operations on October 30, 1949. Previously, street car service had been discontinued on Gordon Street loop between Twelfth and Hamilton streets intersection and North Seventeenth and Chew streets intersection via North

Twelfth, Gordon, and North Seventeenth streets, but the rails remained intact for emergency use. In 1949 the transit company also sold Eighth Street Bridge to the Commonwealth of Pennsylvania.

During April, 1950, Cincinnati, Newport and Convington Railway Company purchased National Power and Light Company's common stock holdings in Lehigh Valley Transit Company and immediately devoted all efforts toward elimination of remaining street railway routes. The transit company also sold Central Park to a real estate investor.

After Philadelphia Division abandoned electric car service between Aineyville Junction and Norristown on September 6, 1951, Lehigh Valley Transit Company transferred all cars to the Allentown Division for disposal. Allentown Division retained the maintenance equipment but assigned all local and limited cars to the scrap list.

## RAILWAY SERVICE ABANDONED

Allentown Division, the only remaining division which operated street railway cars during 1952 and 1953, completed the transit company's conversion from street railway car to autobus operation: Allentown - Greenawalds, June 1, 1952; Allentown-South Bethlehem, October 26, 1952; South Bethlehem-Hellertown, October 26, 1952; Allentown - Fullerton - Catasauqua - Northampton, via Second Street, May 10, 1953; and Allentown-Fullerton via N. Seventh and Washington streets. June 7, 1953. Electric car service ended officially in Allentown and Bethlehem on June 8, 1953, when the last car, No. 912, decorated with patriotically colored bunting and with company officers and officials of both municipalities aboard, operated from Broad and Linden streets, Bethlehem, to Fairview Carbarn, Allentown. Coincidental with conversion of street railway operation to autobus service, Lehigh Valley Transit

Car No. 964, ex-Williamsport Railway Company No. 64, eastbound at Center Square, Allentown, while maintaining the Fairview Loop schedule, circa 1950.
(WR Nos. 60-64, Brill, 1928; LVT Nos. 960-964, 1935)

Bethlehem-bound No. 955 moves along Hamilton Street at 14th Street in Allentown's residential section, July, 1951.
(Nos. 950-959, Brill, 1930)

Company succeeded Lehigh Valley Transportation Company and Easton and South Bethlehem Transportation Company as operators of motorized service.

Between November 14, 1951, and June 12, 1953, Lehigh Valley Transit Company scrapped one hundred and forty-one cars of various types at Bethlehem Steel Company's Bethlehem Plant. A temporary spur which projected from the Bethlehem-Hellertown route on Daly Avenue into the steel plant allowed convenient delivery of cars on wheels. Most cars operated to their destruction under their own power but several, incapacitated by mechanical or electrical failures, required assistance from a tow car. Line car No. R3, with veteran motorman Orville S. Kulp at the controls, operated to the steel plant via the Allentown-Bethlehem northside route on June 12, 1953, and recorded the last electric street car movement over trackage located in the Lehigh River valley of eastern Pennsylvania.

Two cars, Philadelphia Division's interurban limited car No. 1030, which had been sold to Seashore Electric Railway Company's operating trolley museum located near Kennebunkport, Maine, and freight car No. C15, former Liberty Bell Route interurban passenger car No. 808, which had been sold to Philadelphia Transportation Company's Broad Street subway system for utility use, represent the only cars which escaped destruction by the scrap program.

Effective summer, 1953, and continuing for several months thereafter, the various municipalities, through which street railway service had operated, commenced removal of the street railway's physical evidence. Linemen removed overhead wire, feeder lines, and poles; mechanical equipment ripped most rails from street paving; and machines covered either remaining rails or broken paved surfaces. With the conclusion of railway service, Lehigh Valley Transit Company completed the two-year program which converted Fairview Carbarn into Fairview Garage.

Allentown-bound car No. 914 crosses bridge which spanned Lehigh River from Catasauqua to West Catasauqua, summer, 1952.

LVT's city-suburban cars being reduced to metal scrap by fire at scrap preparation division of Bethlehem Steel Corporation's Bethlehem Plant, summer, 1953.

# PHILADELPHIA DIVISION

## ROUTE FORMED

Lehigh Valley Traction Company's southward move from Allentown toward Philadelphia and from Philadelphia to New York collided with Quakertown Traction Company's ambitious expansion plans which projected toward both Allentown and Philadelphia. Quakertown Traction Company, chartered on November 27, 1896, opened three and one-half miles of wide gauge trackage (five feet, two and one-half inches) in Bucks County between Richlandtown and Quakertown on June 11, 1898, and from Quakertown to Perkasie on August 13, 1898. The company's variety of cars, painted either green or red, operated from a carbarn built eastward from Philadelphia and Reading Railway Company's Bethlehem Branch near Quakertown station. A powerhouse located on the site generated electric power. Quakertown and Eastern Railroad Company's refusal to allow the traction company to physically cross their main line southwestward from Richlandtown compelled the traction company to separately operate trackage northeastward from the railroad's right of way and to construct a small carbarn parallel to the track.

Lehigh Valley Traction Company, although not financially capable of completing their own Allentown-Philadelphia project, thwarted Quakertown Traction Company's expansion plans in both northward and southward directions with two strategic maneuvers. First, President Albert L. Johnson supported the construction of Inland Traction Company from a point located near Quakertown Traction Company's southern terminus in Perkasie to Philadelphia (Erdenheim) via Sellersville, Telford, Souderton, Hatfield, Lansdale, and North Wales. Mr. Hugh Crilly, an Allentown contractor and business associate of Mr. Johnson, chartered the new company on November 1, 1898,

and established headquarters in Souderton. Second, Mr. Johnson chartered Allentown and Coopersburg Street Railway Company on September 9, 1899, and acquired operating privileges between Allentown and Coopersburg.

Inland Traction Company inaugurated service from Perkasie to Lansdale over wide gauge right of way with two double truck Duplex cars on April 23, 1900, and from Lansdale to North Wales on October 21, 1900, but temporarily delayed construction of North Wales - Erdenheim trackage. Inland Traction Company's cars, painted red and white, operated from a small carbarn located in the northeast section of Souderton. A spur which projected southward from the main route served the carbarn. The powerhouse located at the carbarn site generated power for the system.

## ST. LOUIS CARS PURCHASED

While the feud with Quakertown Traction Company raged, Mr. Johnson prematurely ordered seventy-five double truck heavy deck roof street railway cars Nos. 137-211 from St. Louis Car Company. The cars, painted Broadway yellow, cream, and silver, measured forty-five feet, six inches in length, and generally reflected a composite of Chicago City Railway Company and Milwaukee Electric Railway Company styles. Interior partitions included two drop platforms and a large coach section which contained twenty-six double rattan walkover seats. A coal heater replaced one seat during winter months. Both platforms were equipped with control and braking systems (later, the company converted eight cars to single end operation).

Mr. Johnson successfully established basic plans for the Allentown-Philadelphia route through various maneuvers: acquired Allentown and Coopersburg Turnpike, the most accessible route

Quakertown Traction Company's car No. 3 stands in Quakertown, circa, 1898.
**(Nos. 2 and 3, St. Louis, 1896; LVT Nos. 110 and 111, 1902)**

The contractor who built Inland Traction Company used an unidentified horse car, probably from a Philadelphia system, to string overhead wire. The crew works southward from Sellersville, circa, 1900.

over Lehigh, or South, Mountain at Summit Lawn, February 5, 1901; acquired controlling interest of Chestnut Hill and Springhouse Turnpike, February 5, 1901; and formed Philadelphia and Lehigh Valley Traction Company by merging Allentown and Coopersburg Street Railway Company and Inland Traction Company, February 15, 1901. The latter arrangement also included the transfer of Inland Traction Company's eleven cars of various types to Lehigh Valley Traction Company's roster. Although the new railway company had been awarded operating privileges through Quakertown, Mr. Johnson considered the acquisition of Quakertown Traction Company's entire property to be more practical. Plans for the Philadelphia-New York route progressed more slowly as compared to the Allentown-Philadelphia project although Mr. Johnson concluded many arrangements with municipalities and railway companies in New Jersey and Pennsylvania between Philadelphia and Perth Amboy. The Philadelphia-New York route had been officially chartered on April 4, 1901, as Philadelphia, Trenton and New York Railroad Company.

During spring, 1901, while St. Louis cars arrived in Allentown from the builder, Philadelphia and New York divisions' opposition organized. The Philadelphia and Reading Railway Company feared competition for local passenger service along Bethlehem Branch and The Pennsylvania Railroad recognized the threat of competition for passenger and freight services between Philadelphia and New York. Accordingly, both railroad companies defiantly refused either crossing or underpassing privileges of their main line right of ways and branch lines. Philadelphia traction magnates, realizing a potential threat to their control over sundry companies which formed the vast Philadelphia city system, joined the opposition. However, Albert L. Johnson's untimely death on July 2,

1901, presaged his railway empire's ultimate collapse. Mr. Robert E. Wright, the Allentown attorney who succeeded Mr. Johnson as president, cancelled the Philadelphia-New York project but approved completion of the Allentown-Philadelphia route.

Physical formation of the Allentown-Philadelphia route southward from a junction with Allentown-Emaus-Macungie route in Mountainville concluded with a series of events: Philadelphia and Lehigh Valley Traction Company leased Quakertown Traction Company and Lehigh Valley Traction Company acquired Quakertown Traction Company's ten cars, September 9, 1901; Allentown-Coopersburg service inaugurated with small single truck cars effective December 19, 1901; Coopersburg-Quakertown trackage completed, March 3, 1902, and Allentown-Quakertown service introduced with St. Louis cars, their initial assignment, March 11, 1902; contracts let for construction of small carbarns at Lansdale and Brick Tavern, April 22, 1902; conversion of wide gauge trackage to standard gauge dimensions completed between Richlandtown and North Wales, May 28, 1902; completed, with the exception of physical crossings and either overpasses or underpasses involving certain routes owned by The Pennsylvania Railroad and Philadelphia and Reading Railway Company, standard gauge track construction between North Wales and Erdenheim, June 5, 1902; Montgomery County court overruled objections of railroads on September 9, 1902, and permitted the traction company's overpassing or underpassing of railroads; bridge over Philadelphia and Reading Railway Company's Bethlehem Branch at North Wales completed, November 23, 1902; and either in late April or early May, 1903, Philadelphia and Lehigh Valley Traction Company's track crew at night "stole the crossing" of Plymouth Branch at Flourtown by installing crossover trackage without Philadelphia and Reading

45

Inland Traction Company's car No. 1 stands at Menlo Park, Perkasie, shortly after the route had been opened for service, circa, 1900.
**(Nos. 1 and 2, Duplex, 1900; LVT Nos. 112 and 113, 1902)**

View of Inland Traction Company's carbarn in Souderton, circa, 1900.

Railway Company's knowledge or consent and operating a St. Louis car over it before witnesses. Coincidental with establishment of railway service which consumed three hours of operating time between Allentown and Erdenheim, Souderton Carbarn became the route's operation and dispatching center for all passenger and utility service.

This belated but successful action by the traction company established continuous service between Sixth and Hamilton streets, Allentown, and Erdenheim. Although trackage physically terminated outside Philadelphia's boundary, the traction company and its successor officially referred to the location as either Philadelphia or Chestnut Hill. Philadelphia's traction investors, by citing charter clauses, prevented Philadelphia and Lehigh Valley Traction Company's physical entrance into Philadelphia.

Time, efforts, and costs expended by the traction company's officials to establish this new service created an unstable financial situation. On May 1, 1903, the finance officer defaulted payment due on Philadelphia and Lehigh Valley Traction Company's bonds, and on May 3, 1903, the Albert L. Johnson Estate applied for receivers in United States District Court in Philadelphia. Accordingly, the court appointed a receivership committee. Despite unfavorable financial conditions, the traction company maintained its scheduled service. Timetables issued May 16, 1903, listed daily hourly Allentown-Chestnut Hill schedules from 6:00 a.m. until 11:00 p.m. At Chestnut Hill passengers travelling to Philadelphia's business district usually patronized nearby Union Traction Company's street railway service which cost only five cents. As an alternative, passengers patronized the nearby faster but more expensive steam railway service offered by Philadelphia and Reading Railway Company and The Pennsylvania Railroad.

Lehigh Valley Traction Company's financial problems reached the inevitable disastrous climax and the receivership committee placed all properties on public sale. Mr. William F. Harrity, representing most receivership committee members at the sale conducted on the Lehigh County courthouse steps in Allentown on June 13, and again on June 20, 1905, purchased all properties for three million, two hundred and seventy-five thousand dollars. The reorganized properties commenced operating as Lehigh Valley Transit Company effective November 3, 1905.

Lehigh Valley Transit Company immediately inaugurated a program arranged to correct and adjust adverse conditions along the Allentown-Philadelphia route, or Philadelphia Division as designated after reorganization. On February 17, 1906, the transit company and Philadelphia Rapid Transit Company announced plans for construction of a new station in Erdenheim eastward from the famous Bethlehem Pike. The structure, when completed, provided terminal facilities for both companies, protected waiting room accommodations for passengers, a covered walkway between cars of both companies, and adjacent land provided a storage area for Lehigh Valley Transit Company's cars. During summer, 1906, in accordance with plans to provide more electric power and to improve transmission facilities, line department crews placed poles for the stringing of a hightension line along the Philadelphia Division preliminary to construction of new substations at Coopersburg, Sellersville, Souderton, Lansdale, and Ambler. By March, 1908, crews had completed assignments.

## LIBERTY BELL ROUTE

Election of R. P. Stevens to Lehigh Valley Transit Company's presidency on July 7, 1907, prepared the company's ascendancy to the position as one of the outstanding electric railway properties in eastern United States.

47

Lehigh Valley Traction Company's car No. 52, assigned to the second section of Quakertown-Richlandtown operations, smashed through Richlandtown Carbarn, circa, 1905.

Sprinkler car No. 1 stands before Souderton Carbarn, circa, 1905.

Operational improvements introduced by Mr. Stevens gradually converted the Philadelphia Division from a long rural route into a modern high speed electric railway system. Allentown-Chestnut Hill schedules adopted December 1, 1907, for the first time advertised the Philadelphia Division as Liberty Bell Route. Most track mileage paralleled, at various distances between Erdenheim and Quakertown, the Bethlehem Pike over which patriots hauled the famous bell in 1777 to safety in Zion's Reformed Church in Allentown while British soldiers occupied Philadelphia.

During autumn, 1907, the Bucks County court, because Quakertown and Eastern Railroad Company had indefinitely suspended operations, permitted the transit company to physically cross the railroad's main line near Richlandtown. As a result, the transit company dismantled the small wooden carbarn which had been constructed parallel to the railroad's right of way and introduced continuous Quakertown-Richlandtown service.

Lehigh Valley Transit Company inaugurated Chestnut Hill - Delaware Water Gap summer excursion service on July 17, 1908, and established a profitable and popular venture. The first "Delaware Water Gap Limited" left Chestnut Hill station in Erdenheim at 9:30 a.m. on a six hour and forty minute schedule to the vacation resort. The transit company assigned St. Louis cars Nos. 177 and 182 specifically to the new service and added more suitable passenger accommodations to both cars for the long journey. Innovations included black leather seats with arm rests; baggage racks; carpeted floor; iced drinking water facilities; a uniformed guide, who by use of a megaphone, provided a factual commentary as the trip passed historical and industrial locations; and a more elaborate Liberty Bell Limited sign painted in green and gold colors. Lavatory facilities had been installed in all St. Louis cars assigned to Allentown-Philadelphia service in 1905.

Subsequent Delaware Water Gap excursion schedules varied from season to season as well as within the same season. At first the St. Louis cars equipped with steam locomotive type pilots, hampered by clearance difficulties, operated only as far as Nazareth. Northward from Nazareth the excursionists proceeded to the gap via Slate Belt Electric Railway Company's cars between Nazareth and Bangor; Bangor and Portland Traction Company's cars between Bangor and Portland; and by either steam trains, autobus (1910), or electric cars of Stroudsburg, Water Gap, and Portland Railway Company (1911) between Portland and the resort area. Circa 1912 St. Louis cars equipped with Providence fenders operated the entire distance between Chestnut Hill and Portland. Dinner arrangements also varied. At one time or another passengers dined during scheduled stops in hotels located either in Allentown, Rittersville (East Allentown), Bethlehem, or Nazareth.

The transit company introduced door-to-door trolley freight service over Philadelphia Division effective Tuesday, October 20, 1908, and to other routes shortly thereafter. Between 1908 and 1951 the transit company operated twenty sundry type cars which had been either built in company shops, purchased, or converted from other types for the special service. During a brief period in 1915 Philadelphia Division unsuccessfully experimented with the operation of freight trailer cars in trains with motor cars. Freight service, like passenger patronage, diminished when highway vehicles offered serious competition commencing in 1927. The company challenged competitors by replacing electric car service along Allentown Division's rural and suburban routes with a pick-up and delivery service operated by auto trucks. Main line service over Easton and Philadelphia divisions continued in the established manner.

**Howard P. Sell Collection**
Montgomery Traction Company's car No. 10 stands before the carbarn located at West Point, circa, 1905.
**(MTC Nos. 8 and 10, Stephenson, 1902; LVT Nos. 411 and 412, 1912)**

**Howard P. Sell Collection**
Allentown-bound limited car No. 186, equipped with steam locomotive-type pilot, moves along Bethlehem Pike northward from Flourtown, circa, 1909.
**(Nos. 137-186, St. Louis, 1901)**

Lehigh Valley Transit Company's officials constantly strove to improve operating conditions along the Liberty Bell Route and sought means to advertise the service. In 1909 the company distributed a well composed and illustrated booklet entitled **A Little Trip Through History**. Basically, the text briefly discussed historical and industrial backgrounds of areas lying adjacent to trackage from Chestnut Hill through Allentown to Delaware Water Gap. Appropriate photographs provided visual evidence of topics presented.

A news item which appeared in the Friday, April 1, 1910, edition of the Philadelphia **Evening Bulletin** unofficially revealed Lehigh Valley Transit Company's future policy for modernization of Liberty Bell Route services. E. B. Smith and Company, one of the transit company's financial backers, announced its purchase of Philadelphia and Western Railway Company, a third rail electric system which had been opened May 22, 1907, between 69th Street, Upper Darby, and Strafford, and predicted a physical connection between both companies and establishment of high speed interurban service with pullman-type cars between Allentown and Upper Darby. Engineers located the junction point near Villanova after investigating several other areas; however, Philadelphia and Western Railway Company agreed to construct and operate the connecting route between Villanova and Norristown and Lehigh Valley Transit Company the route stemming from a junction with their main line near Lansdale to Norristown. Both companies immediately formed plans to quickly conclude their respective projects.

Lehigh Valley Transit Company diligently embarked upon an extensive and costly program which ultimately modernized Philadelphia Division's local and limited services. Between 1910 and 1913 the rehabilitation program, which cost almost five million dollars,

erected a heavy plate viaduct across Trout Creek meadows and Philadelphia and Reading Railway Company's East Penn Yard and main line in South Allentown in place of a spindly truss type structure erected in 1893; eliminated two curves at Aineyville, or Bethlehem, Junction and constructed one curve and straight trackage; eliminated two curves at Emaus Junction and constructed a sweeping curve; revised and relocated trackage between Summit Lawn and Lanark; relocated Rosedale-Quakertown trackage from roadside to private right of way; relocated trackage northward from Perkasie and from Perkasie streets to a direct route after boring a tunnel through Philadelphia and Reading Railway Company's high right of way fill at Perkasie; relocated Perkasie-Sellersville and Sellersville-Derstines track from streets and roadside to private right of way; relocated Souderton-Lansdale track from roadside to private right of way; constructed the new Lansdale-Norristown route from a point southward from Lansdale to a physical connection with Philadelphia and Western Railway Company in Norristown; established Wales Junction, the meeting point of the old and new routes; eliminated the double horseshoe curve in Ambler; installed a track circuit block signal system from Emaus Junction to Brush Siding located near Norristown; placed Hoeschen warning signals at dangerous rural crossings; constructed passenger and freight stations in various towns; and installed a telephone dispatching system and Egry train order registers in siding boxes enroute and connected station, carbarn, and substation telephones with the dispatching system. Trackage revision and modernization eliminated the small carbarns located in Brick Tavern and near Lansdale and established operating time between Allentown and 69th Street Terminal at one hour and fifty-eight minutes.

As part of the new arrangement the surface trackage which connected Phil-

Passenger car No. 802, purchased especially for high speed Allentown-Philadelphia service, stands at 14th Street Carbarn, Allentown, August, 1912.
(Nos. 800-805, Jewett, 1912)

Freight car No. C5, designed for high speed Liberty Bell Route operations, stands on North Front Street, Allentown, after being unloaded from a railroad car in Riverside Yard, summer, 1913.
(Nos. C5-7, Jewett, 1913)

adelphia and Western Railway Company and Lehigh Valley Transit Company within Norristown Borough limits had been separately chartered on July 22, 1910, as Norristown Transit Company with both companies listed as equal owners. Philadelphia and Western Railway Company withdrew from the arrangement in 1942 and transferred its share to Lehigh Valley Transit Company.

Trackage between Quakertown and Perkasie, part of leased Quakertown Traction Company's system incorporated into the main line, proved inadequate for high speed operation of heavy interurban passenger and freight cars. Consequently, Lehigh Valley Transit Company informed the Quakertown Traction Company's stockholders on September 8, 1910, that it intended to terminate the lease and to construct another route from a point located near Red Lion Junction through Quakertown to Perkasie. The stockholders, fearing isolation of their trackage, unhesitatingly sold controlling interest to Lehigh Valley Transit Company in spring, 1911. Subsequently, the transit company rehabilitated trackage and revised curves and sidings where necessary.

Lehigh Valley Transit Company's trolley freight service reached a terminus in Philadelphia's business mart from Chestnut Hill on October 24, 1910, after an agreement had been concluded with Philadelphia Rapid Transit Company. The Philadelphia organization's freight cars moved consignments between Chestnut Hill freight station and a freight house located at Second and Market streets near the dock area.

Lehigh Valley Transit Company concluded successful negotiations for the purchase of Montgomery Traction Company on October 25, 1911, in order to acquire an entrance into Norristown. The twelve-mile wide gauge route between Lansdale and Norristown had been opened in September, 1902. Or-

iginally the company had been chartered as Lansdale and Norristown Electric Railway Company on January 23, 1901. After the formal transfer of property dated January 18, 1912, Lehigh Valley Transit Company abandoned all of the right of way except a one and one-half mile section which paralleled DeKalb Highway northeastward from Norristown and assigned four cars, two single truck and two double truck closed railroad roof types, to Allentown Division's roster. Montgomery Traction Company's cars, painted green with a tan trim, had operated from the carbarn located at West Point. The site also included the powerhouse.

## 800 SERIES CARS PURCHASED

President R. P. Stevens ordered six heavy composite railroad roof combine cars Nos. 800-805 on February 10, 1912, from Jewett Car Company, Newark, Ohio, for assignment to the new high speed service. The cars' interior included five sections: baggage, smoker, coach, lavatory, and vestibule. Although equipped with control and brake systems at both ends, the cars had been generally recognized as a single end type with the baggage end designated as the operating section. Felt insulation placed between double floors eliminated objectionable noises from high powered motors which had been installed in large heavy trucks. Double high back plush walkover seats provided interior comfort for passengers, and colored glass upper sash arch windows added to the cars' magnificence. The six new cars arrived at Riverside Yard, Allentown, in mid-August, 1912.

Philadelphia and Western Railway Company completed their portion of the revised Liberty Bell Route from Villanova Junction to Norristown on August 20, 1912, and inaugurated service on August 26, 1912. In Norristown the cars, by means of a trolley pole and wheel, operated on Norristown Transit Company's tracks for ap-

LVT freight car No. C1 and PRT freight car No. F5 exchange commodity at Chestnut Hill terminal, May 22, 1914.
**(No. C1, LVT, 1908, built from a railroad box car)**

Private interurban car No. 999 stands before 14th Street Carbarn, Allentown, September, 1914.
**(No. 999, LVT, 1914, built over frame of St. Louis car No. 159)**

54

proximately one hundred feet from the north end of the viaduct to the street level station located on Swede Street opposite Montgomery County courthouse.

Lehigh Valley Transit Company, after three years of planning and construction, approached the inaugural date of high speed pullman-type electric interurban railway service between Allentown and Philadelphia. Shortly before midnight, Wednesday, December 4, 1912, construction crews completed the last obstacle, the underpass of Philadelphia and Reading Railway Company's Stony Creek Branch near Lansdale. The transit company conducted test trips throughout the following day, timed to proposed regular schedules, to acclimate all personnel with physical characteristics of both cars and right of way. Without formal ceremony car No. 800 departed from Sixth and Hamilton streets, Allentown, at 7:00 a.m., Thursday, December 12, 1912, with approximately forty passengers aboard and inaugurated two hour and fifteen minute limited service between Allentown and 69th Street Terminal located in Upper Darby six-tenths of one mile westward from Philadelphia's boundary. Twenty-four minutes later the first Allentown-bound car departed from the terminal. Limited cars served only stations enroute but local cars served both station and intra-station stops. A ticket office located on the south side of Hamilton Street eastward from Sixth Street accommodated patrons in Allentown's business district and Philadelphia and Western Railway Company's ticket agents served patrons in 69th Street Terminal.

Union, or 69th Street, Terminal represented the terminal point for various systems: Philadelphia Rapid Transit Company's high speed subway-elevated system which extended to and through Philadelphia's business district; Philadelphia and Western Railway Company which served suburban areas between Upper Darby and Strafford and Upper Darby and Norristown; and Philadelphia and West Chester Traction Company which offered convenient railway service to West Chester and several western suburbs of Philadelphia.

Philadelphia and Western Railway Company drafted an arrangement which allowed Lehigh Valley Transit Company's operation to and from 69th Street Terminal. Philadelphia and Western Railway Company assumed complete responsibility for Lehigh Valley Transit Company's cars over their trackage in return for all revenues collected; in comparison, Lehigh Valley Transit Company, by supplying the car, derived increased increments from patronage attracted by the direct high speed service. A wye constructed eastward from the right of way near the terminal provided reversal facilities for 800 Series cars. When Lehigh Valley Transit Company's cars entered or left the third rail system at the north end of the elevated structure in Norristown, trackside devices automatically lowered or raised all third rail shoes. Crews, however, manually changed power switches and either raised or lowered trolley poles.

Simultaneously with the opening of the new route southward from Lansdale, Lehigh Valley Transit Company built a tower in the crotch of Wales Junction for Philadelphia Division's dispatcher and reclassified the Wales Junction-Chestnut Hill section as a local operation. Introduction of 800 Series cars also established Allentown as the starting and terminating point for Liberty Bell Route limited schedules but Souderton Carbarn continued as the local operations' center. The 14th Street Carbarn located in northwest Allentown serviced 800 Series cars after each trip. Company officials demanded meticulous grooming of 800 Series cars in Allentown between trips. Charwomen cleaned the interior while shop crews filled the water tank, installed new brake shoes and trolley wheels

Cars Nos. 803, 804, and 805, coupled in a three car train, stand on 8th Street Bridge, Allentown, for publicity photograph in 1919.

Car No. 812, converted from car No. 999, stands at 14th Street Carbarn, Allentown, 1921.
(No. 812, converted from No. 999 by LVT, 1921)

(later, shoes), and examined underside equipment from the inspection pit.

Continuous track circuit automatic block signals, timetables, and train orders issued in accordance with standard interurban rules, governed all Philadelphia Division movements. Extra movements displayed either two white flags or lamps and later, all but the last section of scheduled trains displayed either two green flags or lamps at the front end. All cars carried two red Adlake oil signal lamps, lighted only at night, in the No. 2 end's sockets. Timetable rules required a report when entering and leaving the division at Emaus Junction (Emmaus Junction), entering and leaving at Norristown, and reversing direction from a midpoint destination.

Lehigh Valley Transit Company retained the popular Liberty Bell Route designation and symbol for the revised route to 69th Street Terminal although track mileage located either on or adjacent to Bethlehem Pike had been reduced. Philadelphia and Western Railway Company's trackage passed six miles eastward from Valley Forge, site of General George Washington's winter camp for the Continental Army during British occupation of Philadelphia in 1777-1778; continental troops patrolled the area through which Philadelphia and Western Railway Company's right of way had been located; and schedules commenced and terminated in Allentown near Zion Reformed Church tower below which the Liberty Bell had been safely concealed from the British Army.

Enthusiastic public response accorded the new service tremendously pleased the transit company's officials. Within one month holiday and weekend passenger traffic had increased fifty-nine percent. Accordingly, President Stevens telegraphed Jewett Car Company on January 3, 1913, and ordered six additional slightly revised cars Nos. 806-811.

As a measure for more convenience to patrons, the transit company introduced a numbered stop system for Philadelphia Division local service effective February 6, 1913. Line crews fastened white painted boards, two feet by one foot in dimension and bearing black letters and numbers six inches in height, to power line poles at appropriate locations. Stops were numbered consecutively from No. 1, Chestnut Hill, to No. 127, Emaus Junction (Emmaus Junction), and from No. 128, Wales Junction, to No. 141, Norristown Borough line.

Liberty Bell Route's freight service as well as passenger accommodations received the attention of company officials. During March, 1913, three large wooden body Jewett-built freight cars Nos. C5-7, six feet shorter than 800 Series cars but equipped with identical electrical and mechanical equipment, arrived at Riverside Yard, Allentown, to operate the high speed freight service planned between Allentown and 72nd Street freight terminal near Philadelphia and Western Railway Company's carbarn. This service, plus auto truck operation to and from shippers and receivers in Philadelphia, replaced the previous arrangement with Philadelphia Rapid Transit Company at Erdenheim (Chestnut Hill).

As a further move toward establishing the Philadelphia Division as a first class interurban system, official regulations required a standard garb for all passenger crew members effective April 1, 1913. Motormen, until 1932, dressed in white and indigo striped overalls and coats with nickel buttons and dark blue visor caps with silver piping and conductors wore blue serge uniforms with brass buttons and blue visor caps with gold piping. An appropriate bar representing one year and a star for each five year period sewn on the left sleeve near the shoulder indicated the employee's length of service. Other furnishings remained the employees' choice.

57

View of Souderton Carbarn, circa, 1921.

Rail-bond test car No. 500 stands at 14th Street Carbarn, Allentown, circa, 1923. The transit company revised snow plow No. 519 for the service in 1916. Although the car served all divisions it operated over Philadelphia Division more frequently.

Lehigh Valley Transit Company cancelled continuous Chestnut Hill-Delaware Water Gap excursion service operated by St. Louis cars before the 1913 vacation season opened. Instead, new publicity suggested patronage of 800 Series cars between 69th Street Terminal and Allentown; St. Louis cars between Allentown and Portland; and Stroudsburg, Water Gap and Portland Railway Company's cars between Portland and the gap. Allentown Division crews manned St. Louis cars assigned to two daily round trips between Allentown and Portland. The operation lasted two seasons.

Maintenance crews unloaded car bodies Nos. 806-811 as they arrived at Riverside Yard, Allentown, from the builder during the first week of July, 1913, and immediately placed them on Brill trucks already equipped with third rail accessories. The cars' structure and mechanical and electrical systems included minor improvements as compared to cars Nos. 800 to 805. The mechanical staff at 14th Street Shop also incorporated certain innovations of the new group of cars into the older group in order to standardize operations, maintenance, and equipment inventories.

Right of way improvements between Zion Hill and Souderton, the 1910-1912 rehabilitation program's final section, progressed sufficiently to permit initial operation of two 800 Series cars in a train between Allentown and 69th Street Terminal on Saturday, August 30, 1913, to facilitate voluminous Labor Day weekend traffic movements. The successful venture established standard two-car train practice.

Opening of Eighth Street Bridge across Lehigh Creek valley from Allentown's business district to South Allentown on November 18, 1913, caused the relocation of the transit company's center of operations in Allentown from Sixth to Eighth and Hamilton streets intersection. Liberty Bell Route limited and local cars operated in both directions over the structure after Eighth and Hamilton streets intersection had been designated by the transit company as both the starting and terminal point of all limited and most local services scheduled by the Philadelphia Division.

Mr. Harrison R. Fehr, Mr. R. P. Stevens' successor elected in July, 1913, authorized construction of an elaborate double truck arch roof private interurban car to attract charter service and to serve as an official car on special occasions. During November, 1913, Lehigh Valley Transit Company towed smashed St. Louis car No. 159 from Hecktown Carbarn storage to 14th Street Shop to provide the base and frame for the car to which the No. 999 indentification had been assigned. Shop crews completed No. 999 on September 5, 1914. Interior subdivisions included two motorman cabs, dining room complete with furniture and service facilities, fully equipped kitchen, lavatory, and club room. No. 999, during assignments to the Liberty Bell Route, usually appeared as the second car in a train with an 800 Series car but elsewhere it operated singly. Former United States President William Howard Taft and Governor Martin G. Brumbaugh of Pennsylvania represented No. 999's most distinguished passengers.

Roadway improvements and opening of Eighth Street Bridge by early 1914 reduced one way limited schedules over the Liberty Bell Route from two hours and fifteen minutes to one hour and fifty-eight minutes. The new arrangement, in addition to the elevated-subway trip in Philadelphia, separated Allentown and Philadelphia business districts by two hours and fifteen minutes and replaced steam railroad service as the main artery between both cities. One Philadelphia business man referred to the Liberty Bell Route as "The Prosperity Trail".

Lehigh Valley Transit Company

Richlandtown local car enroute to LVT's Quakertown station crosses over Reading Company's Bethlehem Branch and Quakertown and Bethlehem Railroad's main line in Quakertown, circa, 1924.

Center entrance interurban car No. 708 enters Souderton Carbarn after concluding operation of a Liberty Bell Route local schedule, circa, 1925.
(Nos. 700-711, Southern, 1916)

opened modern Fairview Carbarn in South Allentown on May 18, 1914, as the center of Allentown Division's operations and Philadelphia Division's limited service. Loop trackage built near the entrance located at Lehigh Street permitted the reversal of the Liberty Bell Route's cars' operating, or baggage, end after each northbound trip in preparation for the next southbound trip. Previously, crews automatically positioned the cars by operating over Gordon Street loop trackage between 14th Street Carbarn and the station located at either Sixth and Hamilton streets or Eighth and Hamilton streets.

After careful study and planning cars Nos. 809, 810, and 811 successfully completed a three car train round trip test operation over the entire Liberty Bell Route on July 31, 1914. As the result of this satisfactory venture, the company built additional power substations at Summit Lawn, Quakertown, and Souderton and regularly operated three car passenger trains on weekends and holidays until 1935. Three car freight trains appeared shortly thereafter and operated as late as 1951.

Officials of Lehigh Valley Transit Company utilized modern methods to publicize Liberty Bell Route services. In 1914 all of Allentown's movie theatres projected a one thousand foot thirty-five millimeter film entitled **A Honeymoon Trip to Delaware Water Gap**. The film, prepared for the transit company by a professional organization, followed honeymooner's journey from downtown Philadelphia, through 69th Street Terminal, to the front door of a resort hotel located on Delaware River's right bank in Delaware Water Gap. The film ended with the couple alighting from a Stroudsburg, Water Gap and Portland Railway Company car at their destination. The film footage also included sundry views of the Liberty Bell Route and 800 Series cars; Allentown Fair Grounds; Allentown's business district; and Lehigh Valley

area's industrial plants. In addition and in conjunction with Philadelphia and Western Railway Company, the transit company published free of charge for several months beginning in 1914, a monthly magazine entitled **Transit**. The format included schedules offered by both companies and connecting routes; discussions concerning safety; municipal histories; industrial reviews; and advertisements.

Liberty Bell Route's local passenger service also grew at a gratifying rate and by early 1915 required additional cars for more frequent high speed service. The transit company solved the problem momentarily by converting nine St. Louis cars to train operations by installing lightweight Westinghouse couplers and SME airbrake equipment. During June the traffic department adopted schedules in which St. Louis cars operated in trains between Allentown and Wales Junction and, after separation at that point, singly between the junction and Norristown and the junction and Chestnut Hill. St. Louis car train operations proved inadequate and ended with the introduction of 700 Series local cars in late summer, 1916.

Lehigh Valley Transit Company concluded its fifteen-year conflict with Quakertown Traction Company on December 31, 1915, by acquiring sole ownership of stock and by absorbing the entire property into its main organization. The transaction had been consumated without altering Philadelphia Division policies.

### 700 SERIES CARS PURCHASED

President H. R. Fehr and Superintendent Branson collaborated and designed a large steel center entrance arch roof universal car intended for use in city, local interurban, and, by virtue of multiple unit controls and couplers, main line interurban limited train services. Interior subdivisions included coach, smoker, lavatory, and

Chair car No. 710 stands on P&W's third rail trackage in 69th Street Terminal, Upper Darby, circa, 1930.
**(Nos. 703, 706, and 710 converted to chair car, LVT, 1922-1923)**

Deluxe limited car Nos. 703 stands at 17th and Chew Streets, Allentown, for publicity photograph, April, 1931.
**(Nos. 702, 703, 704, and 710 converted to Deluxe type, LVT, 1931)**

two motorman cabs. The car, heated by a coal stove system along one side and electric heaters along the other, seated fifty passengers by utilizing additional temporary facilities. After receipt of the order on June 1, 1916, Southern Car Company, High Point, North Carolina, built twelve cars, according to the design, to which the transit company assigned the 700 Series classification. Cars Nos. 700-711 gradually assumed Allentown-Chestnut Hill hourly local service between August 30, and September 30, 1916, and replaced all but ten St. Louis cars entered on Souderton Carbarn's roster. Thereafter, St. Louis cars handled Quakertown-Richlandtown assignments, half hour main line local service, and spare service. Allentown Division acquired excess St. Louis cars from Philadelphia Division.

Lehigh Valley Transit Company's officials, utilizing 700 Series cars' flexibility, between 1916 and 1931 regularly assigned them to Liberty Bell Route limited schedules on weekends and holidays either as a two car train or as a third car in a train with two 800 Series cars. During 700 Series cars' main line limited assignments, St. Louis cars entered on Allentown Division's roster served as substitutes and operated all hourly local service schedules.

Decline of patronage along the Quakertown-Richlandtown local route after World War I required an economy adjustment. Effective April 14, 1919, the transit company introduced one man service over the route, and shortly thereafter Allentown Division's 14th Street Shop adjusted lightweight double truck cars Nos. 195 and 206 for permanent assignment to this operation in place of St. Louis cars. Other 187 Series cars served as substitutes whenever necessary.

Miller trolley shoes, or slides, gradually replaced trolley wheels on 800 Series cars after successful experiments

on Easton Transit Company's 214 Series steel lightweight interurban cars in 1916. Slides improved current collection, reduced arcing, and eliminated schedule interruptions caused by the shattering of trolley wheels during maximum speed operations. By January, 1921, all Philadelphia Division local, limited, freight, and utility cars had been similarly equipped. As the result of slide usage the trolley wire required a special grease coating to prevent friction wear. For this unusual service, the company altered and equipped lightweight passenger car No. 189 with additional air compressors and grease containers. Copper tubing and hose extended from grease receptacles placed inside the car through the roof and along both poles to the slides. Both poles (the front turned rearward), one for lubrication and the other for current collection, were raised during greasing operations. As the car moved slowly over Philadelphia Division trackage once per month the apparatus discharged a thin lubricant mixture onto the wire. In 1937 former Easton Transit Company passenger car No. 211 replaced No. 189, and in 1949 emergency car No. 79 replaced No. 211.

Discontinuance of official service assignments, lack of charter service applications, and increase of main line passenger service dictated private car No. 999's conversion to passenger car No. 812. The car, revised in 14th Street Shop, Allentown, operated its initial Liberty Bell Route passenger service assignment on July 4, 1921. No. 812, until 1932, operated only occasionally as a single car but appeared often as either the second or third car in trains with 800 Series cars in weekend and holiday service. Transit company officials regarded the car's lesser seating capacity and uncomfortable riding qualities, as compared to 800 Series cars, to be unsuitable for regular service operation.

Allentown-bound car No. 800 accommodates passengers at Quaker-town station, September 7, 1936. LVT revised the car in early 1936 for one man service.

Philadelphia-bound No. 700 ascends the northern slope of Lehigh, or South, Mountain, May 1, 1937.
**(Nos. 700, 701, and 711 revised for one man service, LVT, 1932)**

## CHAIR CAR SERVICE INTRODUCED

Beginning May, 1922, Lehigh Valley Transit Company converted, at intervals, center entrance cars Nos. 703, 706, and 710 into straight side chair cars. Effective February 7, 1923, and continuing until April, 1931, for an extra fifty cent fare, later reduced to twenty-five cents, the Liberty Bell Route offered chair car accommodations. A chair car appeared in a train with an 800 Series car for daily except Sunday trips of **The Philadelphian** leaving Allentown at 8:00 a.m. and 4:00 p.m.; **The Allentonian** leaving 69th Street Terminal at 8:57 a.m. and 3:57 p.m.; and for Philadelphia theatre patrons, the Wednesday and Saturday only **The Midnighter** leaving 69th Street Terminal at 12:15 a.m. Thirteen wicker chairs, later replaced by plush upholstered revolving chairs, eight in the coach section and five in the smoker, or observation, compartment comprised the seating capacity. White LVT monogrammed cloths covered the head rest and back of each chair. The body alterations left the control positions unchanged and intact.

Lehigh Valley Transit Company altered Liberty Bell Route operations during the mid-1920's when privately owned automobile operations initially competed seriously with public transportation service: abandoned Telford Junction-Telford local trackage, a remnant spur of the original route which had remained after the 1902 revision, and constructed Telford station along the main line, February 27, 1925; opened newly constructed main line trackage along private right of way between Rosedale and a point located northward from Center Valley and abandoned the old route which followed the public highway between both locations, September 2, 1925; and abandoned Wales Junction-Chestnut Hill trackage and substituted autobus service, July 31, 1926. Simultaneously, with the abandonment of Wales Junction-Chestnut Hill trackage the tran-sit company assigned the nine center entrance 700 Series cars to a newly created Allentown - Norristown local schedule, dismantled Wales Junction tower, and moved Philadelphia Division's dispatcher into Allentown Division's dispatching headquarters located in Fairview Carbarn. St. Louis cars which remained on Souderton Carbarn's roster operated short intra-division local assignments which varied periodically according to patronage requirements.

Mile-a-minute interurban operations, improved public roads, and increased use of closed automobiles by the mid-1920's combined to produce serious and fatal crossing accidents between Allentown and Norristown. Mechanical department crews replaced the discordant two-whistle warning combination on passenger and freight cars with loud blaring twin Strombos air horns beginning November 2, 1927. However, the far carrying distinctive warning sound, signs, flashing crossing lights, ringing bells, and swinging arms failed in their purpose and the rash of crossing accidents continued.

Movement of empty freight cars from Allentown to Upper Darby freight terminal in trains with 800 Series cars operating regular passenger schedules, a convenience plan introduced in autumn, 1927, became standard practice in 1928 for economic reasons and continued throughout 700 Series cars' operation until 1939. Loaded freight cars, either single units or trains, usually returned to Allentown during the following morning before commencement of passenger service.

Company management introduced a modified paint scheme for all cars in 1928. A dark red varnished body; silver striping, medium size numbers, monogram, anticlimbers, headlight, and roof replaced the bright red, gold, tan, and black combination adopted in 1917. Effective with the new colors, painters stenciled "Allentown, Liberty

65

Philadelphia-bound car No. 706 enters Gehman Siding, located southward from Souderton, May 2, 1938.

Cincinnati and Lake Erie Railroad Company's car No. 414 stands on a railroad car in Riverside Yard, Allentown, September 25, 1938.
**(C&LE Nos. 413, 414, 112, and 115, Cincinnati, 1930; LVT Nos. 1020-1023, 1938-1939)**

Bell Route, Philadelphia" in large silver letters on 800 Series cars' letterboards. Previously, from 1912 until 1918 the words "Philadelphia, Allentown, and Water Gap" appeared in small letters on the body's lower portion at the baggage entrance and "Liberty Bell Route" at the passenger entrance; from 1918 until 1923 "Liberty Bell Route" at the baggage entrance and "Philadelphia, Norristown, Allentown, Bethlehem, and Easton at the passenger entrance; and from 1923 until 1928 only "Liberty Bell Route" at the passenger entrance.

The Quakertown-Richlandtown route, the portion of Quakertown Traction Company's original route which had not been incorporated into the Liberty Bell Route's main line, concluded street car service and commenced autobus operations effective June 15, 1929. Shortly thereafter the transit company sold the autobus franchise to a private company.

A third rail equipment short circuit set ablaze and partially destroyed car No. 811 on September 1, 1929, near Philadelphia and Western Railway Company's Villanova Junction and thereby reduced the 800 Series car roster from twelve to eleven cars. The scorched steel skeleton stood on trucks in Fairview Carbarn yard until Allentown Division scrapped obsolete equipment during 1934 and 1935.

Lehigh Valley Transit Company and Reading Company, recognizing the threat of private autobus competition to railway service offered by Liberty Bell Route and Bethlehem Branch respectively, inaugurated joint Allentown-Philadelphia autobus service effective March 8, 1931. The service, basically arranged to thwart competitors, offered only negligible accommodations.

Lehigh Valley Transit Company and many other interurban systems throughout the United States suffered financial setbacks in the late 1920's and early 1930's and passed from the "golden years" into a declining era. Widespread unemployment and competition from privately owned automobiles diminished revenues. Accordingly, Lehigh Valley Transit Company established one man operation for Philadelphia Division local service only effective January 25, 1931, and immediately replaced the two man operated 700 Series center entrance cars at Souderton Carbarn with twelve St. Louis cars transferred from Allentown Division's roster.

## DELUXE SERVICE INAUGURATED

Lehigh Valley Transit Company, planning substitution of all less power consuming rebuilt 700 Series cars for the heavy 800 Series cars in limited service, revised straight side chair cars Nos. 703 and 710 and converted center entrance cars Nos. 702 and 704 into a straight side type identified as "Deluxe Limiteds". Removal of center entrance structural beams and plates, coal heater, interior partitions, and doors reduced total weight from thirty-five to thirty-three net tons, or eight tons lighter than an 800 Series car, and addition of motor field taps increased maximum speed to seventy miles per hour, or approximately ten miles per hour faster than an 800 Series car. Deluxe interior improvements included a left hand control operating position, double high back stationary forward facing cushioned leather seats, wall bracket lighting, electric heating, curtain draped side windows, a new ceiling and roof ventilator system, and an observation lounge outfitted with individual chairs, sofa, card table, and table lights. Chair car No. 706, temporarily converted into a parlor car outfitted with rows of revolving chairs removed from chair cars, served as a substitute.

One hundred percent 800 Series limited car operation, introduced in 1912, ended on the Liberty Bell Route on Sunday, April 26, 1931, when the "Deluxe Limiteds", maintaining a fast

Southbound car No. 700 in a train with a freight motor car enter the north end of Quakertown Siding, December 11, 1938.

Southbound cars Nos. 1021 and 1000 halted at Summit Lawn for minor adjustments during trial run, February 2, 1939.
**(C&LE Nos. 125, 128, 126, 121, 127, 123, 129, 120 and 122, Cincinnati, 1930; LVT Nos. 1000-1008, 1938-1939)**

one hour and forty minute schedule which served only seven station stops, commenced operating 8:00 a.m. and 4:00 p.m. southbound and 8:57 a.m. and 3:57 p.m. northbound trips. Although 800 Series cars maintained all other schedules, the transit company's publicity extolled "Deluxe Flyer" performances. Two men comprised the deluxe car crew, but the car's structure revealed a convenient adaptation to one man operation. On November 15, 1931, Lehigh Valley Transit Company transferred deluxe cars to Easton Division and operated the improved service directly between Easton and 69th Street Terminal via Bethlehem and Allentown.

Norristown station relocation effective November 15, 1931, an accommodation arranged particularly for Philadelphia and Western Railway Company's new platform-loading 200 Series "bullet" cars, eliminated the street level station located on Swede Street in favor of a second story station located near the north end of the elevated structure which led to Schuylkill River viaduct. The arrangement also ended Philadelphia and Western Railway Company's street operation in Norristown. As the result of the relocation Lehigh Valley Transit Company's limited cars served the new platform station and street-loading local cars terminated at a separate area constructed on the viaduct several feet northward from the station. Protected walkway facilities constructed along the viaduct from the street level entrance to the station made the latter arrangement possible.

During November, 1931, Lehigh Valley Transit Company suddenly introduced a retrenchment policy and cancelled plans for complete deluxe car operations. Work equipment immediately towed and pushed unfinished cars Nos. 707 and 708 from 14th Street Shop into the storage yard located at 13th and Gordon streets. The cars gradually deteriorated until the company assigned them to the scrap list in 1938.

A crossing collision with an automobile in Hatfield on January 27, 1932, eliminated car No. 810 from the operating roster. The heavy car, derailed by the impact, hurtled down the right of way, ploughed up trackage, and severed two service poles before halting. Maintenance equipment towed the smashed car to Fairview Carbarn and placed it in storage in front of fire-gutted No. 811.

One man operation replaced the Liberty Bell Route's traditional two man limited car crews on August 1, 1932, and the transit company immediately transferred all 800 Series cars from regular to spare service assignments. Deluxe service also ended at the same time and short intra-division schedules replaced Allentown-Norristown hourly local service. Easton Division returned deluxe cars to Fairview Carbarn in Allentown. Henceforth, limited cars served all local stops as well as stations.

A motley group of interurban cars maintained Philadelphia Division limited schedules between 1932 and 1939. Former "Deluxe Limited" cars Nos. 702, 703, 704, and 710; No. 706, former parlor car converted to coach; Nos. 700, 701, and 711, converted to one man service by enclosing center entrance door wells and steps with steel plates and pairs of windows and creating passenger entrances with steps and air operated doors and traps on both sides of the No. 1 end; and No. 812, equipped with air operated doors and traps at passenger entrance for one man service indiscriminately appeared in regular scheduled assignments. All remaining 800 Series cars appeared occasionally either in regular service with the operator stationed at No. 2 end controls or in train service behind 700 Series cars and No. 812.

Lehigh Valley Transit Company's

Philadelphia-bound car No. 812 passes Bryn Mawr station located along Philadelphia and Western Railway Company's third rail system, February 6, 1939.

Car No. 809, operating a regular southbound schedule, stands at Allentown station, February, 1939.
**(Nos. 806-811, Jewett, 1913)**

mechanical department, utilizing the sturdiness of 800 Series cars, replaced two lightweight wooden body freight cars in Philadelphia Division service by converting passenger car No. 802 to freight car No. C14, later renumbered No. C19, during autumn, 1934, and No. 808 into freight car No. C15 in summer, 1935.

A fire, similar to that which had destroyed car No. 811, reduced car No. 703, a deluxe type, to a scorched steel shell near Philadelphia and Western Railway Company's King Manor station on November 18, 1935. Maintenance crews scrapped the remains at Fairview Carbarn several weeks after its removal to Allentown. Lehigh Valley Transit Company immediately converted car No. 800 into a one man type as No. 703's replacement. Alterations included relocating lavatory; removing passenger vestibule and smoking compartment partitions; converting the passenger end to the operating end by installing air operated traps and doors; permanently fastening a headlight on the roof above the train door at the operating end; installing a destination sign box in the lower portion of the right front window; and moving the third rail-overhead changeover switch and air horns to the new operating end. In February, 1936, No. 800, painted dark red with small silver numbers, striping, monograms, anticlimbers, headlight, and roof, assumed regular car status.

A Pennsylvania Utility Commission rule issued early in 1937 required the installation of "dead man" controls on all cars which operated Liberty Bell Route passenger and freight services. William Klein, Superintendent of Equipment, designed the apparatus which the mechanical department quickly installed. An air piston placed near the brake valve, when extended, struck an extension added to the brake lever and moved the lever to emergency position. At the same time sand flowed from boxes to the rails. A second pis-

ton forced the control reset switch to "off" position. Either full brake application or depression of a foot pedal prevented air pressure from activating both pistons.

The transit company, acceding to Allentown council's request in 1938 to void southward movements through the trailing crossover in opposition to northbound automobile traffic on South Eighth Street, routed Liberty Bell Limited cars which had completed a northbound trip back to Fairview Carbarn over Union Street loop via Hamilton, South Sixth, and Union streets to the north entrance of Eighth Street Bridge. The maneuver automatically reversed the car's position for the next southbound trip. Customary northward movements of southbound scheduled cars through the facing point crossover for placement before the station on South Eighth Street remained unchanged.

## 1000 SERIES CARS INTRODUCED

Engineers engaged by Electric Bond and Share Company in 1938 evaluated Lehigh Valley Transit Company's position as a street railway operator and recommended, among other provisions, retention of the Liberty Bell Route and acquisition of newer second hand cars to replace most 700 Series cars. In addition, the proposal suggested the scrapping of several freight cars and all St. Louis and 800 Series cars. Within several weeks the transit company inaugurated the suggested rehabilitation program.

The second hand cars acquired for the modernization program by Utility Equipment Company included eleven single end single unit lightweight compact double truck interurban cars which had inaugurated high speed luxury service over Cincinnati and Lake Erie Railroad Company's network in Ohio in summer, 1930. To this group of cars Lehigh Valley Transit Company assigned the 1000 Series classification.

John P. Scharle

Freight car No. C7, enroute from Easton to Philadelphia, moves westward along Hamilton Street over Jordan Creek bridge in Allentown, May 24, 1939.

John J. Bowman, Jr.

St. Louis car No. 186 stands at Center Valley station prepared for Center Valley-Allentown local schedule, July 9, 1939.

On September 30, 1930, Philadelphia and Western Railway Company had conducted an experimental trip over the entire Liberty Bell Route with Cincinnati and Lake Erie Railroad Company's car No. 127, one of the cars acquired by Lehigh Valley Transit Company during the modernization program.

All eleven cars arrived in Allentown during September and October, 1938, and almost immediately entered the shops for rehabilitation and conversion to the Liberty Bell Route's mode of operation. Major structural changes included the creation of a left front platform-street level entrance and a rear center emergency exit. Mechanical changes included the addition of third rail brackets, beam, and shoe on both sides of both trucks; installation of a trolley pole on the roof above the operating end for reverse movements; covering of open bar pilot with sheets of stainless steel; and fastening of an overhead headlight on the roof above the operating end. Later, the mechanical department authorized minor changes of equipment as the need arose. A new paint scheme identified the "Liberty Bell Limited" cars from city-suburban types: a picador cream body; mountain ash scarlet headlight, letters, numbers, and trim; silver roof and trolley poles; and black wheels and undercarriage. Cars predominantly equipped with Westinghouse products were numbered from 1000 to 1006 and those with General Electric products from 1020 to 1023.

Effective February 13th, six 1000 Series cars commenced operation of regular schedules. Several weeks pssed before the transition from 700-800 Series to 1000 Series car operations had been completed. In order to provide another reversing facility for the single end 1000 Series car, track crews built a loop at dead end Rink Siding in Norristown. Liberty Bell Route patronage increased after the introduction of modern service and Lehigh Val-

ley Transit Company's officials quickly acquired two more cars during April, 1939. The cars, identified as Nos. 1007 and 1008, increased the 1000 Series roster to thirteen entries.

Utility Equipment Company, with whom Lehigh Valley Transit Company had arranged the acquisition of newer second hand cars and scrapping of its older equipment, between 1938 and 1940 scrapped two 800 Series cars, Nos. 803 and 804, and sold four bodies, Nos. 801, 805, 807, and 810, to private individuals for sundry building usage. Lehigh Valley Transit Company retained and converted cars Nos. 800, 806, and 809 into freight cars Nos. C16, C17, and C18 respectively. Basically, the freight cars' structure resembled Nos. C14 and C15 with minor adjustments.

Six of the seven St. Louis cars which remained in operating condition during 1939 received assignments to Philadelphia Division's local schedules until the transit company acquired six of seven medium weight suburban cars which formerly had operated Steubenville, East Liverpool and Beaver Valley Traction Company's service in eastern Ohio near the Pennsylvania boundary. To this group the transit company assigned the 430 Series classification. Fairview Carbarn transferred refurbished 430 Series cars to Souderton Carbarn's roster one at a time between September 14, and November 7, 1939. Originally, Lehigh Valley Transit Company had planned to use Easton Division's 214 Series cars in Philadelphia Division's local service, but the low steps of car No. 217 presented clearance difficulties at Norristown station during a trial trip.

During late summer, 1939, Fairview Carbarn's shop crews moderately reconditioned cars Nos. 701, 702, 704, 710, and 812 for spare service. Reconditioning included reupholstery of seats and painting of the entire interior. The five interurban cars and the six

Allentown-bound local car No. 435 enters School Siding, Center Valley, May 15, 1940.
(SEL&BV Beaver, Stratton, East Liverpool, Midland, Toronto, and Steubenville, Kuhlman, 1927; LVT Nos. 430-435, 1939)

Norristown-bound grease car No. 211 stands in School Siding, Center Valley, August 2, 1940.
(ETCo Nos. 211-213, Brill, 1906; revised as grease car, LVT, 1937)

430 Series cars received an exterior paint scheme similar to the 1100 Series Easton Limited cars: mountain ash scarlet body; white window frames; gold numbers; silver roof and poles; and black trucks and undercarriage. Previously, Utility Equipment Company had scrapped 700 Series center entrance cars Nos. 705, 707, 708, and 709 and sold No. 706's body for conversion to a highway diner. Fairview Carbarn retained the bodies of No. 700 and 711 for several years as yard storage units. In 1947 the transit company painted the four retained 700 Series cars and No. 812 in the same scheme as 1000 Series cars.

Liberty Bell Route operation continued in a normal fashion until fire destroyed car No. 1004 on December 20, 1940, at King Manor station on the Philadelphia and Western Railway Company's third rail system. The conflagration started in the switch box enroute but the operator continued to the station and safely discharged all passengers before the fire blazed out of control and destroyed both car and station. Transit company maintenance crews scrapped No. 1004's remains at Fairview Carbarn in June, 1941, after salvaging various structural shapes.

The transit company fortunately discovered a replacement for car No. 1004 in Indiana where Indiana Railroad Company had retained three lightweight multiple unit type interurban cars for its Indianapolis-Seymour route, the only remnant of a vast railway network. From this group Lehigh Valley Transit Company purchased club car No. 55. Car No. 55 arrived in Allentown on February 25, 1941, and immediately entered Fairview Carbarn for conversion to car No. 1030. Shop crews cleverly adjusted the exterior body structure to resemble the other 1000 Series cars but retained the club car interior arrangement. Interior furnishings included upholstered individual chairs and sofas for thirty passengers; carpeted floor; cloth window curtains; simulated indirect lighting; lavatory facilities; latest magazines; table lamps; and a wall receptacle which contained potted plants. The car operated its first regular scheduled trip over the Liberty Bell Route on October 3, 1941. Disgusted maintenance employees who groomed No. 1030 between every trip, according to special rules, soon nicknamed it "The Golden Calf".

Two serious accidents which occurred along the Liberty Bell Route during July, 1942, caused a degree of defection among patrons. On July 8, northbound passenger car No. 1003 plunged head-on into southbound freight car No. C14 on the long sweeping curve which led from Brush Siding across Brush meadows to DeKalb Highway. Eleven passengers and car No. 1003's motorman died and thirty others suffered injuries as the heavy steel-wood car ripped through the smaller lighter passenger car. Seventeen days later, on July 25, car No. 1001, second section northbound, crashed into the rear end of car No. 1030, first section northbound, stalled in dense foliage on the curve which bordered the east side of Perkasie Park. Fourteen passengers and car No. 1001's motorman suffered injuries but no fatalities resulted. Effective September 20, 1942, the transit company, as a measure to reduce further incidents, introduced a half hour departure schedule which allowed only one car in each signal block and increased scheduled trip time from two hours to two hours and fifteen minutes. Eventually, Fairview Carbarn shops rebuilt cars Nos. 1001, 1030, and C14, renumbered C19, and scrapped car No. 1003.

During World War II the Liberty Bell Route's patronage increased tremendously and required, consequently, the constant assignment of equipment. This condition resulted in the hasty deterioration of the car bodies and motors. Freight car No. C15's crash into the observation end of car No. 1022 on Sep-

John P. Scharle

Philadelphia-bound freight cars Nos. C17 and C5 pass through the cut located westward from Coopersburg, August 4, 1940.

William D. Middleton

Philadelphia-bound car No. 1002, ex-C&LE No. 126, enters the north end of Sellers Siding, February 4, 1950.

tember 13, 1948, at "chicken house" stop located southward from Menlo Park, Perkasie, caused no injuries but revealed the transit company's future plans toward conversion to autobus operations. Shop workers commenced but never completed repairs. A work car moved car No. 1022 into yard storage and shop crews converted club car No. 1030 into an all coach type with the installation of two rows of forward facing double bucket seats.

A drastic policy move further revealed the Liberty Bell Route's progressive plan toward conversion to autobus service. Effective September 24, 1949, Lehigh Valley Transit Company cancelled passenger car operations over Philadelphia and Western Railway Company's tracks between Norristown and 69th Street Terminal and terminated schedules at Norristown station. Thereafter, passengers who required transportation to and from 69th Street Terminal patronized connecting Philadelphia and Western Railway Company's service. Although Liberty Bell Route's passenger service had been severed, freight car operations over the third rail system between 72nd Street freight terminal and Norristown remained unchanged.

### LIBERTY BELL ROUTE ABANDONED

Lehigh Valley Transit Company on Thursday, September 6, 1951, at 6:00 p.m. suddenly announced the conversion of Liberty Bell Route railway service to autobus operation effective with commencement of schedules on September 7, 1951. During the remaining hours of September 6th, the company's operators quickly moved all rolling stock from Liberty Bell Route trackage into storage at Allentown Division's Fairview Carbarn until disposition had been arranged. At 11:06 p.m. car No. 1006 departed from Allentown on the last scheduled passenger car trip over the Liberty Bell Route and returned from Norristown at 2:46 a.m., Friday, September 7, 1951. Unceremoniously Liberty Bell Route's railway service passed into history.

Track crews commenced the removal of Liberty Bell Route track at 8:00 a.m., Friday, September 7th, and by Tuesday, September 11th, had removed track at School Lane, Souderton; Broad Siding, Lansdale; and from Emmaus Junction to Aineyville Junction, Allentown. Motor vehicles aided the Souderton and Lansdale projects and work cars Nos. 522 and 551 aided the latter. During winter, 1951-1952, a scrap company dismantled all other trackage plus overhead wire, signals, crossing lights, and most bridges.

Philadelphia-bound freight cars Nos. C19, C15, and C17 cross P&W's Schuylkill River viaduct, summer, 1951.
(Nos. C14-18, ex-passenger cars Nos. 802, 808, 800, 806, and 809, converted to freight cars by LVT, 1935-1939; No. C14 renumbered No. C19, 1943)

Philadelphia-bound No. 1030 passes an Allentown-bound 1000 Series car in Nace Siding, Souderton-Telford, summer, 1951.
(Indiana RR No. 55, ACF, 1931; LVT No. 1030, 1941)

# EASTON DIVISION

## HORSE CAR OPERATIONS

Easton and South Easton Passenger Railway Company, a horse car system, chartered May 27, 1866, commenced operation as a public carrier in Easton during 1867. Trackage extended southward from Centre Square, junction of Third and Northampton streets, along South Third Street; crossed Lehigh River to South Easton via the public bridge; and followed Canal and Lehigh streets (the latter eventually renamed Valley Street) to Lehigh Valley Railroad Company's shops. Enroute the railway also served Lehigh Valley Railroad Company's passenger station. The street railway company operated from stables and carbarn built on Canal Street between Centre and Lehigh streets.

The West Ward Passenger Railway Company, chartered May 5, 1871, shortly thereafter established east-west street railway service in Easton with horse cars. Trackage extended westward from Centre Square via Northampton, Walnut, and Washington streets to the fairgrounds located at Seventeenth and Washington streets. The company operated from stables and carbarn constructed at Sixteenth and Washington streets. The West Ward Passenger Railway Company reorganized as The West End Passenger Railway Company on October 28, 1884, and on May 31, 1886, merged with Easton and South Easton Passenger Railway Company and formed Easton, South Easton and West End Passenger Railway Company. The new company abandoned the buildings located on Canal Street and combined all operations at the newer facilities located at Sixteenth and Washington streets. Easton's town council granted exclusive trackage rights over all streets to this organization.

Phillipsburg Horse Car Railroad Company, chartered April 9, 1867, opened a standard gauge route three and six-tenths miles in length through Phillipsburg, New Jersey, in 1871. Trackage extended eastward from a turntable located at Union Square via South Main Street to a turntable near Andover Furnace. The Company constructed a carbarn and stables on North Main Street several hundred feet northward from Union Square. In 1885 the railway extended westward from Union Square, Phillipsburg, via the covered bridge which spanned Delaware River to a turntable constructed in the street near the curb in line with East Northampton Street at Centre Square, Easton. Trackage in Easton had been chartered on March 5, 1871, as The Centre Square and Delaware Bridge Passenger Railway Company.

## ELECTRIC SERVICE INAUGURATED AND TRACKAGE EXPANDED

In spring, 1887, D. W. Nevin, acting in behalf of his uncle, Major D. R. B. Nevin of Philadelphia, purchased the Mann farm located in Easton's College Hill section and in June, 1887, contracted with Daft Motor Company of New York for installation of a wide gauge electric trolley car system on the prevailing ten percent grade which rose from a point near Bushkill Creek's left bank to the Mann farm. Construction of the route, chartered as Lafayette Traction Company on January 5, 1887, commenced in summer, 1887. The electric railway company established carbarn facilities on the northwest corner of Burke and Porter streets.

Lafayette Traction Company conducted electric car tests over the route on January 7. 1888, and on January 14, 1888, the first car, one of two single truck closed passenger cars, commenced revenue service between the north end of Bushkill Creek Bridge located on North Third Street and the carbarn via Cattell Street. Operating crews worked

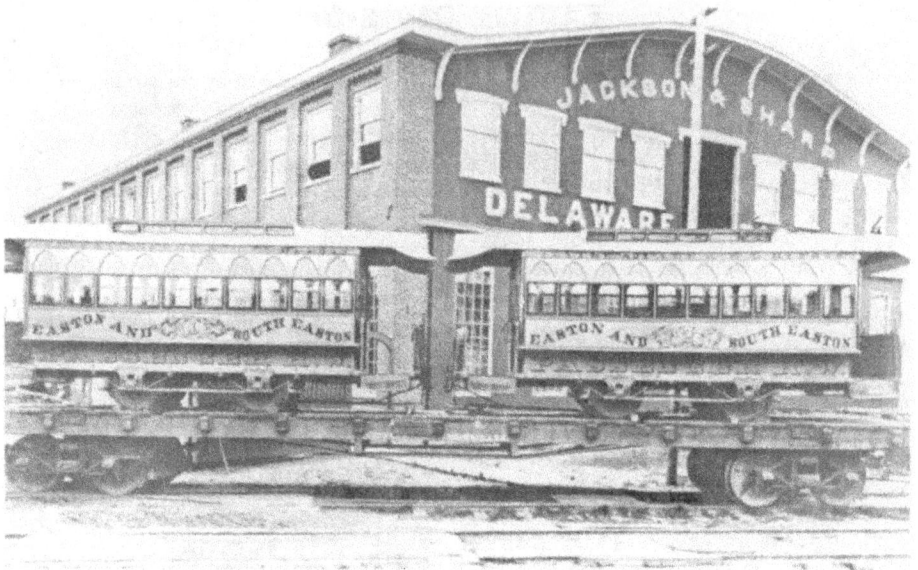

Easton and South Easton Passenger Railway Company's horse cars Nos. 1 and 2 stand before Jackson and Sharp's plant in Wilmington, Delaware, prepared for shipment to Easton, 1867.

A westbound horse car of The West End Passenger Railway Company stands on Northampton Street westward from Centre Square, Easton, circa 1885.

from 6:30 a.m. until 10:00 p.m. six days per week. The route ranks as the third electric street railway to commence operation in the United States.

Electric car service reached Centre Square via North Third Street on July 25, 1888, amid angry protests from residents along the street. In order to establish service before the opposition thoroughly organized, Lafayette Traction Company had laid ties on top of the street southward from Bushkill Creek's right bank and had strung overhead wire removed from the north end of the route. An electric car had dragged it from that point down College Hill to Third Street. Because of the hasty nature of the act, the company had not installed sufficient service poles to hold the wire and consequently improvised by tying the end of the wire to trees growing inside the circle at Centre Square. Also, track had not been laid on the bridge thereby requiring the transfer of passengers from one car to another in order to complete a trip. Residents along North Third Street, incensed by the maneuver, immediately instituted legal action to halt operation of electric cars. Dauphin County court settled the matter by ruling that Lafayette Traction Company's operation of electric cars had invalidated the original charter.

Pennsylvania's state legislature, however, passed another act which permitted the operation of street railway service with electricity. Accordingly, Pennsylvania Motor Company received a charter on November 13, 1888. Meanwhile, in October, 1888, Easton, South Easton and West End Passenger Railway Company, the horse car system, purchased Lafayette Traction Company. In a legal maneuver which settled Easton's street railway problem, the horse car system officially leased the electric railway route to Pennsylvania Motor Company on January 5, 1889, for nine hundred and ninety-nine years. On March 1, 1889, the

company inaugurated electric car service to The Central Railroad Company of New Jersey's station located on 4th Street and on June 20, 1889 from Burke and Porter streets to Shawnee Spring located on Paxinosa Heights (Parker and Shawnee avenues).

The new extensions established electric car service from The Central Railroad Company of New Jersey's station via Centre Square and College Hill to the recreation area located at Shawnee Spring. The horse cars system and the electric railway's route, according to the arrangement, operated on parallel tracks along Northampton Street between Centre Square and Fourth Street with the electric railway company using the north track. On July 16, 1890, the traction company introduced its first summer, or open, car over electrified trackage.

As a means to provide additional safety and mechanical features for the ascent and descent of College Hill, Pennsylvania Motor Company installed a crude counterbalancing cable car arrangement in summer, 1889. A wooden body car loaded with six tons of pig iron, by means of cable, sheaves, and hooks, ran on a track inside a one hundred foot trough constructed along the hillside between Chestnut and Delaware streets. The safety car traveled one foot to the electric car's twelve foot movement. Cars, when ascending the hill, hooked onto the cable at the bottom of the hill and unhooked at the top of the hill and cars which descended reversed the procedure. Schedules had been arranged so that the cable car always remained in the proper position for each movement. On September 25, 1889, the cable car broke loose, descended the hill at a fast rate of speed, smashed into the stone wall located at the end of the trough, and scattered pig iron along the street. Shortly thereafter the traction company abandoned the cable car arrangement.

Officials of Lafayette Traction Company and spectators pose with car No. 1 on College Hill during inauguration of electric railway service, January 14, 1888.
(Nos. 1 and 2, Lewis and Fowler, 1888)

Cars Nos. 42, 41 and 6 of Easton Transit Company stand in Union Square, Phillipsburg, New Jersey, circa 1898. After electrification the company motorized horse cars and converted others to trailers.

## EASTON TRANSIT COMPANY
## ORGANIZED

Easton Transit Company, organized June 30, 1892, represented the consolidation of Easton, South Easton and West End Railway Company and The Center Square and Delaware Bridge Railway Company. The new organization purchased the capital stock of Phillipsburg Horse Car Railroad Company and embarked upon a plan which by December 10, 1892, had electrified all street railways which served Easton except the trackage which extended from Centre Square, Easton, through Phillipsburg. Easton Transit Company converted the stables located at Sixteenth and Washington streets into a carbarn and shops for electric cars and purchased power from the public producer located at Second and Lehigh streets. Additional maneuvers by the company expanded the system in 1893: constructed trackage westward from Walnut Street along Northampton Street to Seventeenth Street and southward along Seventeenth Street to a connection with existing trackage built on Washington Street; in 1892-1893 commenced operation of The Weygadt Mountain Railway, chartered August 3, 1891, under contract with private owners from Shawnee Spring to the mountain's crest; circa 1893 constructed new trackage from Shawnee Spring to Eddyside and to West Easton from Washington Street (both projects operated only for a short duration); leased Pennsylvania Motor Company on March 13, 1893; on July 13, 1894, opened Easton and Bethlehem Transit Company, chartered July 6, 1892, from The Central Railroad Company of New Jersey's station via Dock Street to Island Park with a spur to West Easton; in 1894 converted horse car operations to electrification from Centre Square, Easton, through Phillipsburg and added trackage along North Main Street in Phillipsburg to the residential area expanding on the heights; and created semi-loop trackage in South Easton via Canal, Mauch Chunk, Glendon (Avenue), Charles, St. Joseph, and St. John streets with a switchback safety arrangement constructed on St. Joseph Street. Lightweight electrified horse cars operated over the wooden covered bridge which spanned Delaware River between Easton and Phillipsburg until both communities jointly erected a steel cantilever bridge in 1895. All electric trackage, either leased or owned by Easton Transit Company, had been constructed to the wide, or Pennsylvania, gauge measurement of five feet, two and one-half inches. The company identified its rolling stock with a red and yellow paint scheme.

Easton, Palmer and Bethlehem Street Railway Company, an independent entity, organized on June 11, 1897, and commenced construction of a standard gauge route between Easton and Bethlehem. Trackage extended through North Bethlehem via North Main Street and Elizabeth Avenue from the terminus located in Bethlehem's business district at Broad and Main streets; followed William Penn Highway through farmland to a point located in Palmer Township westward from Easton (crossed Easton and Northern Railroad Company via a high wood bridge); extended northeastward from the highway and across fields to a point near Eighteenth and Ferry streets; and reached a terminus in Easton's business district at Northampton Street via Ferry and Sixth streets. The company established powerhouse, carbarn, and office facilities in Butztown village located along William Penn Highway near Bethlehem. On November 6, 1898, Easton, Palmer and Bethlehem Street Railway Company's maroon painted single truck cars inaugurated service along the entire route. Within Bethlehem's boundaries the new railway company established loop service by using Lehigh Valley Traction Company's tracks along Broad and Linden streets after town council ruled that

Car No. 8 stands on Washington Street near Seventeenth Street in autumn, 1894. The carbarn and yard form the background.
(Nos. 1-10, Brill, 1892)

Summer car No. 23 of Easton Transit Company stands before the station located at Paxinosa Inn on trackage identified as The Weygadt Mountain Railway, 1898.
(Nos. 21-23, ex Nos. 5-7, Rogers-Lamokin, 1893)

both companies would have to share trackage. Lehigh Valley Traction Company, accordingly, scheduled service into North Bethlehem via Elizabeth Avenue and North Main Street.

During summer, 1898, Easton, Palmer and Bethlehem Street Railway Company built Oakland Park, an amusement center, on a ten acre tract of farmland located northward from main line trackage and westward from Farmersville. The small park offered adequate picnic and amusement facilities for residents of both Easton and Bethlehem. During summer months chartered cars conveyed social groups to the park from various points along the route. Private investors acquired the property after World War II and converted the land into a real estate development.

The Northampton Central Street Railway Company, a trackage only system organized to establish Easton-Nazareth street railway service in conjunction with Bethlehem-Easton service, obtained a charter on March 3, 1899. The six-mile standard gauge route extended northward to Nazareth through Palmer Township from Nazareth Junction, later identified as Country Club Junction. The junction point had been located midway between Butztown and Easton along Easton, Palmer and Bethlehem Street Railway Company's trackage. Electric cars inaugurated Easton-Nazareth service in September, 1900, via the new route and on March 20, 1901, physically formed a junction with Slate Belt Electric Street Railway Company's trackage at the intersection of Broad and High streets, Nazareth. Schedules of both companies usually provided a convenient transfer arrangement for patrons, and cars of one system occasionally operated over the other's tracks.

## EASTON CONSOLIDATED ELECTRIC COMPANY

Easton Consolidated Electric Company, incorporated March 10, 1899,

acquired, either by purchases of capital stock or by lease, the following electric railway properties: Easton, Palmer and Bethlehem Street Railway Company; Easton and Bethlehem Transit Company; Easton Transit Company; Pennsylvania Motor Company; The Northampton Central Street Railway Company; and Phillipsburg Horse Car Company. Easton Transit Company became the control unit of the combination and all rolling stock carried Easton Transit Company's identifications and yellow and red paint scheme.

Easton Transit Company opened a short spur southward from Butztown to Freemansburg on March 17, 1900, under the corporate identification of The Freemansburg Street Railway Company. Lehigh Valley Traction Company, planning to enter Freemansburg via the southern boundary, battled Easton Transit Company for permission to construct trackage on Main Street. After each company threatened to lay track on opposite sides of the street near the curb, borough council wisely decreed that both companies would have to share one track. When Easton Transit Company failed to receive crossing privileges over The Central Railroad Company of New Jersey's main line which skirted the west and north sides of the borough, Lehigh Valley Traction Company built a route from a junction with their South Bethlehem-Hellertown route in Northampton Heights through Freemansburg to a terminus located southward from the railroad track directly opposite Easton Transit Company's terminus. Lehigh Valley Traction Company inaugurated service to Freemansburg with single truck cars on October 30, 1901.

Easton Consolidated Electric Company, meanwhile, authorized construction of a modern carbarn on the railway property located at Sixteenth and Washington streets on October 8, 1900. The area, approximately two city squares in size, represented the electric

Easton, Palmer and Bethlehem Street Railway Company No. 21,
enroute to Easton from Bethlehem halted along William Penn Highway for
photograph, circa 1899.
(Nos. 11-29, oddly, Newburyport, 1898)

Car No. 66 operates on Bethlehem-Easton route near Butztown,
circa 1905.
(No. 66, Brill, 1892; ex No. 10)

railway's center and included office, repair shop, storage building, freight house, maintenance yard, and car storage yard. Butztown Carbarn continued as center of standard gauge car operations and Phillipsburg Carbarn as an operational and service center for cars assigned to Phillipsburg operations.

## LEHIGH VALLEY TRACTION COMPANY LEASES EASTON COMPANIES

Albert L. Johnson, president of Lehigh Valley Traction Company, leased all properties under Easton Consolidated Electric Company's control effective December 1, 1900, as part of a program designed to create an electric railway empire in eastern United States. After the lease had been concluded, Lehigh Valley Traction Company's cars entered Easton via standard gauge track and Easton Transit Company's standard gauge cars entered Allentown. In addition, cars from one company appeared in the service of the other. Because all trackage under control of Easton Consolidated Electric Company, except that built by Easton, Palmer and Bethlehem Street Railway Company, had been constructed in the wide gauge dimension, complete coordination of operations between Lehigh Valley Traction Company and the Easton systems had been impossible. Accordingly, on July 21, 1901, Easton Consolidated Electric Company approved reduction of the gauge to standard dimensions on all routes except Phillipsburg Horse Car Railroad Company's trackage. By 1904 track crews had completed the assignment. After conversion of track gauge, Butztown Carbarn became a storage unit.

Albert L. Johnson's sudden death in July, 1902, cancelled plans for the electric railway empire. His organization ultimately experienced financial difficulties and entered receivership in May, 1903. Payment of cash interest due Easton Consolidated Electric Company according to terms of the lease

could not be met in May, 1903, but the lessor accepted the permanent transfer of four St. Louis cars from Lehigh Valley Traction Company's roster to Easton Transit Company's roster in lieu of cash payment. However, when a cash payment could not be arranged in spring, 1904, the Easton company sought and received on May 2, 1904, the return of all properties which had been leased plus an equal number of cars involved in the original transaction but not necessarily the same cars.

Easton Consolidated Electric Company, after resuming operation of its property, charged that Lehigh Valley Traction Company had not properly maintained either cars or track. Consequently, officials commenced a rehabilitation and expansion program: purchased three new lightweight double truck deck roof cars Nos. 105-107 for assignment to Easton-Bethlehem service, 1904; formed connected circular trackage at Centre Square, 1904; on April 21, 1905, contracted for the construction of a bridge from Lehigh River's left bank to Island Park, an amusement center, and established loop trackage and a station on the island; elected Harrison R. Fehr as president to guide the new organization, May 19, 1905; and completed plans to underpass trackage of Easton and Northern Railroad Company in Palmer Township along the Easton-Bethlehem route, September 5, 1905.

Easton Transit Company purchased land lying northward from Freemansburg in February, 1906, and in April commenced construction of a tunnel underneath The Central Railroad Company of New Jersey's main line trackage. After the tunnel had been completed, Easton Transit Company effected a physical connection with Lehigh Valley Transit Company (successor to Lehigh Valley Traction Company in 1905) in Freemansburg. Next, Easton Transit Company extended trackage from Walnut and Washington streets intersection

Car No. 90 stands before Easton Carbarn on February 25, 1913.
(No. 90, Brill, 1898, ex EP&B No. 20)

Easton Limited car No. 214 stands at 14th Street Carbarn of Lehigh
Valley Transit Company, Allentown, circa 1918, after rehabilitation dur-
ing the modernization program.
(Nos. 214, Brill, 1914)

in Easton along Butler Street, Freemansburg Avenue, private right of way, and along the public highway to Middletown (Miller Heights) and a junction with Butztown-Freemansburg trackage under the style of Easton and South Bethlehem Transit Company (chartered May 19, 1906, as successor to The Freemansburg Street Railway Company). In South Bethlehem, Easton Transit Company laid track along Fourth Street from a junction with Lehigh Valley Transit Company at the Daly Avenue ramp of Northampton Heights bridge to a stub end terminus at New Street. A controversy with the church located at Fourth and Taylor streets caused the construction of trackage on Webster, Fifth, and Polk streets until the church relented in 1914 and approved the laying of track on Fourth Street between Webster and Polk streets.

Easton Transit Company, by operating over Lehigh Valley Transit Company's track between Freemansburg and Northampton Heights, inaugurated direct Easton-South Bethlehem service on December 30, 1908, although service along the Easton-Middletown section had been established on June 15, 1907. In preparation for Easton-South Bethlehem service, the Easton company purchased six lightweight double truck cars Nos. 208-213 and renumbered double truck cars Nos. 105-107 to 205-207. As part of the plan to provide adequate accommodations, Lehigh Valley Transit Company and Easton Transit Company agreed to an arrangement which transferred the control of all regular service over Northampton Heights-Freemansburg trackage to the latter company but allowed cars of the former to serve the shops of Bethlehem Steel Company, which lay adjacent to and northward from the right of way, during shift changes.

Two projects completed eastward from Phillipsburg, New Jersey, concluded the transit company's trackage

expansion and established peak route mileage at fifty-one miles: from the original terminus located near Phillipsburg's eastern boundary to a point near Lehigh Valley Railroad Company's station in Alpha, 1906; and from the terminus of North Main Street route to Ingersoll-Rand Company's plant, 1907. Second track, sidings, and connections accounted for five additional miles of trackage.

Signing of the trolley freight car law by Pennsylvania's governor in 1907 evoked no particular enthusiasm from Easton Transit Company. Subsequently, the company offered adequate but not outstanding freight car service over most of its routes. A small single truck passenger car, converted to haul freight, accommodated shippers and receivers.

In a corporate maneuver Easton Transit Company replaced Easton Consolidated Electric Company as controlling body of the Easton-Phillipsburg street railway systems effective January 3, 1908. In the process Easton Transit Company, already owners of Phillipsburg Horse Car Railroad Company and Easton and Bethlehem Transit Company and lessor of Pennsylvania Motor Company, absorbed Easton, Palmer and Bethlehem Street Railway Company and Northampton Central Street Railway Company into the main organization. On February 10, 1909, Easton Transit Company also absorbed Easton and South Bethlehem Transit Company.

Easton Transit Company and predecessor organizations by 1909 had purchased sixty-one single truck open type and forty-seven closed cars and had acquired, via leases, thirty single truck cars of various types. Only nine cars purchased between 1904 and 1907 represented the large double truck type. The transit company continued the consecutive numbering policy for rolling stock in preference to the series system. Seven of the open cars represented a trailer type used exclusively for Island

Single truck car No. 402, formerly summer car No. 95, rebuilt as a closed center entrance car in 1917, photographed for equipment record purposes, circa 1920.

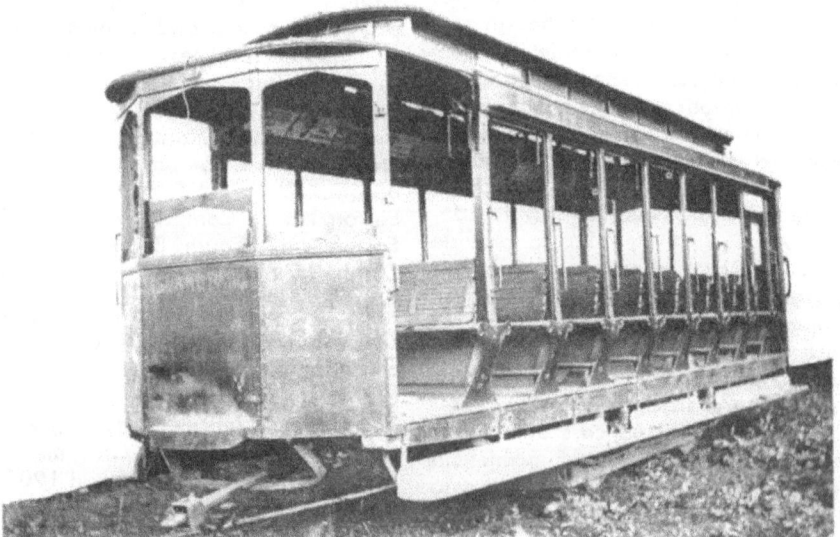

Former Island Park route trailer No. 35 photographed as part of the modernization program's publicity in 1920.
(Nos. 27-39, oddly, purchased from Wilkes-Barre Railways, 1906)

Park-Centre Square service during summer months between 1906 and World War I.

## PROPERTY REVITALIZED

Easton Transit Company, maintaining favoritism for single truck cars for city operation, purchased eighteen closed single truck arch roof cars between 1911 and 1914. Twelve standard gauge cars identified as Nos. 300-311 operated in Easton city service and six wide gauge cars identified as Nos. 170-175 operated in Phillipsburg. The latter group, although identified with Easton Transit Company's red and yellow paint scheme and ETCo monogram, also designated Phillipsburg Horse Car Railroad Company as owner by means of a small metal plate fastened on the body. Coincidental with the purchase of new cars the company introduced its ETCo monogram.

The year 1913 marked several significant events in Easton Transit Company's history: commenced changing of wide gauge trackage in New Jersey to standard gauge dimensions, a chore completed in 1914; converted trucks of wide gauge cars to standard gauge size; eliminated switchback trackage on St. Joseph Street and Charles Street in South Easton and created a loop by constructing new trackage along St. John Street to a connection with original trackage on Berwick Street; established Allentown-Bethlehem-Easton limited service in conjunction with Lehigh Valley Transit Company, March 17, 1913; and on July 1, 1913, Lehigh Valley Transit Company acquired controlling shares of Easton Consolidated Electric Company's stock. Conversion of wide gauge trackage to standard gauge dimensions in New Jersey transferred Phillipsburg Carbarn's status from an operating unit into a storage unit, and, accordingly, cars assigned to service in New Jersey communities operated from the main carbarn in Easton. A few months later the transit company replaced the conventional manual signal system with the United Signal Company's automatic type along city routes and the Nachod type along rural areas westward from Easton.

Effective March, 1915, Easton Transit Company placed into regular service on the Easton-South Bethlehem route the first of ten multiple unit medium weight double truck arch roof suburban-interurban cars purchased periodically through 1916 from The J. G. Brill Company in Philadelphia. The group of ten cars, identified as Nos. 214-223, represented the last new cars purchased by the company. Acquisition of these cars changed the standard paint scheme from yellow and red combination to a bright red, gold, tan, and black scheme. Later, the assignment of the 214 Series cars to Allentown-Bethlehem-Easton limited service caused adoption of a train order dispatching operation in conjunction with the Nachod signal system between Wilson Borough and Bethlehem. In addition, Allentown-Bethlehem-Easton limited schedules co-ordinated in both directions with Allentown-Philadelphia limited schedules so that patrons could travel between Philadelphia and Easton with a minimum delay in transfer time.

Meanwhile, as part of the revitalization of railway properties, Phillipsburg Horse Car Railroad Company reorganized on October 11, 1916, and changed its corporate title to a more modern name — Phillipsburg Transit Company.

Significant events accomplished during the period preceding World War I included both trackage abandonments and formulation of a project which would have added more track miles and established improved service. In 1915 the transit company and owners of Paxinosa Inn abrogated the contract for operation of The Weygadt Mountain Railway and consequently the transit company terminated service over the College Hill route beyond Parker Avenue. At approximately the

Car No. 219, maintaining the Easton-Bethlehem-Allentown limited schedules stands in the northeast corner of Centre Square, Easton, circa 1930.
**(Nos. 218-223, Brill, 1916)**

Lightweight city-suburban car No. 213 stands on Washington Street near Easton Carbarn, circa 1930.

same time the company constructed a physical junction with Lehigh Valley Transit Company at Fourth and New streets, Bethlehem. Mr. Harrison R. Fehr, president of both Lehigh Valley Transit Company and Easton Transit Company effective 1913, in spring, 1916, allocated one million dollars to double track the Easton-Bethlehem route; double track the Liberty Bell Route between Allentown and Norristown; construct a new interurban route between Bethlehem and a junction with the Liberty Bell Route at Center Valley; and purchase four heavy allcoach interurban cars for high speed operation between Center Valley and Easton via Bethlehem. Double tracking of the Easton-Bethlehem right of way had been completed from Wilson Borough to Taylor-Wharton Company's plant when United States' entry into World War I cancelled further revisions. After hostilities ceased, Electric Bond and Share Company, manager of Lehigh Valley Transit Company's properties effective July, 1917, abolished the project. Meanwhile, Easton Transit Company conducted another moderate equipment modernization program and converted sixteen single truck open cars to closed types with four representing the center entrance variety.

Lehigh Valley Transit Company, accepting funds available to the transportation industry from federal agencies in 1917, purchased twenty-four steel arch roof double truck city-suburban type center entrance cars from The J. G. Brill Company in Philadelphia. To this group the transit company assigned the 900 Series classification. After receipt of the cars, Lehigh Valley Transit Company immediately transferred cars Nos. 920-923 to Easton Transit Company's roster for assignment to Easton-South Easton service. For many months, other than numbers, the four cars carried no identifications of either company.

Between 1919 and 1923 Lehigh Valley Transit Company conducted an extensive modernization program which rehabilitated most of the rolling stock assigned to Allentown and Philadelphia divisions and to Easton Transit Company. Easton Transit Company's cars were the first to be processed in Allentown Division's 14th Street Shop. Adjustments included, among others, general body repairs and installation of mechanical doors and steps. Although transit officials confidently viewed future operations, signs of degeneration gradually appeared. Easton Transit Company abandoned trackage between Glendon (north end of Glendon-Easton bridge) to Island Park in 1920 and from Country Club Junction to Nazareth on July 20, 1920.

## PROPERTY BECOMES EASTON DIVISION OF LVT

After Easton Transit Company's rehabilitation program had been completed, Lehigh Valley Transit Company, the majority stockholder, leased Easton Transit Company for ninety-nine years effective March 1, 1922, and designated the property as Easton Division. Subsequently, Lehigh Valley Transit Company's red, tan, gold, and black paint scheme and LVT scroll monogram replaced ETCo identifications. Although a duplication of numbers involved certain cars assigned to Allentown, Philadelphia, and Easton divisions as the result of the lease, Lehigh Valley Transit Company never renumbered the cars involved. By leasing Easton Transit Company, Lehigh Valley Transit Company acquired eighty-eight passenger cars and ten utility cars of various types.

Between 1922 and 1939 Lehigh Valley Transit Company frequently transferred cars from Allentown Division to Easton Division's roster. Double truck 137 Series St. Louis, 187 Series double truck semi-convertible, 400 Series single truck, 600 Series double truck convertible; 900 Series center entrance double

93

Deteriorating St. Louis car No. 182, transferred from Allentown Division to Easton Division for substitute city and interurban service, stands before Easton Carbarn, November 13, 1938.
(Nos. 137-186, St. Louis, 1901)

Easton Limited car No. 1100, posed for publicity photograph, stands in the reversal loop at Fairview Carbarn, Allentown, December, 1938.
(Dayton & Troy Nos. 201-204, Cincinnati, 1928; LVT Nos. 1100-1103, 1938)

94

truck; and, later, 900 Series end entrance converted double truck cars supplemented Easton Division's roster. St. Louis cars usually served the Allentown-Easton limited route and other types maintained city-suburban schedules.

In 1927 Easton Division's city routes became a one man operation along with those in Allentown, but a two man crew continued to handle cars assigned to the Allentown-Bethlehem-Easton limited route until 1932. Easton Carbarn's mechanical staff adjusted city cars for one man accommodations. In 1928 the transit company slightly revised the limited car route in Bethlehem. Thereafter, limited cars operated between Browns Siding and Broad and Linden streets intersection via Pembroke, Minsi Trail Junction, and Broad Street in place of the original arrangement through Edgeboro along Easton Avenue. The transit company provided service to the Edgeboro section of Bethlehem by extending the Easton-South Bethlehem schedules through Bethlehem's business district.

During the late 1920's and early 1930's the privately owned automobile and unemployment among working forces compelled electric street railway companies to either curtail or abandon service. Easton Division, accordingly, systematically abandoned trackage: Glendon and West Easton to Fourth and Northampton streets, Easton, 1927; Ferry Street from Eighteenth Street to Walnut Street, Easton, 1928; Centre Square, Easton, through Phillipsburg to Alpha, New Jersey, and from Union Square, Phillipsburg, to Ingersoll-Rand Company via North Main Street, October 31, 1931; from Broad and Main street, Bethlehem, to Browns Siding via Main Street, Elizabeth Avenue and Easton Avenue, June 1, 1932; Butztown to Miller Heights and from Freemansburg Road, Wilson Borough, to Northampton Heights, Bethlehem, via Freemansburg, June 1, 1932; and tracks removed on Northampton

Heights bridge, Bethlehem, in 1936 but Allentown Division used track from the bridge's west end to Fourth and New streets for steel work's service until July 13, 1939. Lehigh Valley Transportation Company's autobus service replaced most of the abandoned railway operations, but Easton-South Bethlehem autobus service had been chartered separately as Easton and South Bethlehem Transportation Company on June 8, 1932.

Coincidental with reduction of Easton Division's track mileage, Lehigh Valley Transit Company transferred most of Allentown Division's cars back to Fairview Carbarn, Allentown. However, either one or two 137 Series cars remained at Easton Carbarn until 1939 as replacement for 214 Series cars assigned to Allentown-Bethlehem-Easton limited service. The curtailment of services also caused the removal of one of the two tracks constructed around Centre Square, Easton, and scrapping of excess cars of all types except 214 Series cars. In accordance with the curtailment program, the company also sold Butztown and Phillipsburg carbarns to private organizations.

Commencing November, 1931, and continuing until August, 1932, Lehigh Valley Transit Company offered direct high speed interurban service between Easton and Philadelphia's western suburbs without inconveniencing passengers with a change of cars. Deluxe Limited service had been originally established over the Liberty Bell Route from Alentown to Upper Darby in April, 1931. The transit company transferred the four deluxe type 700 Series cars from Philadelphia Division's roster to Easton Division's roster with the change of schedules. Easton Division crews operated deluxe cars between Easton and Allentown twice daily in place of the hourly schedules normally maintained by 214 Series cars; however, Philadelphia Division crews manned the cars between Allentown and Nor-

Car No. 223, operating South Easton Loop service, stands on Berwick Street at Glendon Avenue, May 12, 1939.

Allentown-bound freight car No. C5 approaches the Pembroke section of Bethlehem near the present Stefko Boulevard and Fleming Street intersection, May 12, 1939.
(Nos. C5-7, Jewett, 1913)

ristown. Lehigh Valley Transit Company discontinued deluxe service over the Liberty Bell Route in August, 1932; transferred the four cars back to Philadelphia Division's roster; and reassigned 214 Series cars to Easton-Allentown schedules which had been maintained by deluxe cars.

## CITY RAILWAY ROUTES
## ABANDONED

A group of engineers selected by Electric Bond and Share Company studied Lehigh Valley Transit Company's entire railway property early in 1938 and recommended, among other provisions, retention of Easton-Bethlehem-Allentown interurban service and conversion of all Easton city routes to autobus service. At the time of the study Easton Division's city routes served Freemansburg Road via Washington and Walnut streets; Easton Hospital via Northampton Street; College Hill; and South Easton. Lehigh Valley Transit Company, through Utility Equipment Company, acquired four second hand modern lightweight interurban cars, which had previously served Dayton and Troy Electric Railway Company in Ohio, for Easton-Bethlehem-Allentown service. The cars, built by Cincinnati Car Company in 1930, had been identified by the electric railway industry as the curved-side type.

Dayton and Troy Electric Railway Company cars Nos. 201-204 arrived on railroad flat cars at Riverside Yard, Allentown, during September, 1938. Renovations by Allentown Division's 14th Street Shop included enclosement of right rear door; removal of lavatory located near left rear side; repainting interior and reupholstering of seats in velour fabric; conversion of rear platform into a semi-lounge arrangement equipped with individual revolving chairs; installation of an overhead headlight on front roof crown; installation of a trolley pole and accessory equipment at front end; and covering spoke

pilot under front platform with stainless steel sheets. The exterior color scheme included a mountain ash scarlet body with white stripe; gold numbers and "Easton Limited" painted on letterboard along both sides; silver poles; and black undercarriage. Lehigh Valley Transit Company identified the cars as Nos. 1100-1103 in accordance with the established series numbering policy. From February 4, to February 6, 1939, the company exhibited one car in the business district of Allentown, Bethlehem, and Easton. The four refurbished cars replaced 214 Series cars in revenue service between Easton and Allentown effective February 8, 1939. The 214 Series cars continued to operate Wilson Borough-Easton-South Easton service after removal from interurban service and appeared in limited service only in emergencies.

Easton Division's phase of the modernization program ended Sunday, November 5, 1939, with discontinuance of street railway car operations over city routes. Autobuses of Lehigh Valley Transportation Company commenced operation of service on the following Monday over most streets formerly served by street cars with variations, and Easton's track removal program commenced shortly thereafter. Track for limited car operations remained on Lehigh Street between Twenty-first and Seventeenth streets; on Seventeenth Street between Lehigh and Washington streets; on Washington Street between Seventeenth and Walnut streets; along Walnut Street between Washington and Northampton streets; and on Northampton Street between Walnut Street and Centre Square. The latter arrangement included double track on Northampton Street and the circle through the square. The four 1100 Series cars remained on Easton Division's roster along with six utility cars of various types; however, the company transferred all ten 214 Series cars, one work car, and one snow sweeper to Allentown Division's roster. The

97

Randolph L. Kulp

Car No. 223, operating South Easton Loop service, ascends Smith Avenue hill, November 3, 1939. Lehigh Valley Railroad Company buildings form the background.

Industrial Photo Service

Car No. 308 stands at the terminus of the College Hill route at Parker Avenue and Shawnee Drive, November 4, 1939. Lengthening shadows symbolized the railway's imminent abandonment.
(Nos. 303-308, Brill, 1912)

latter retained all but two 214 Series cars for spare service. Easton Division meanwhile either scrapped or sold all other cars for utility purposes. One double truck lightweight passenger car, No. 211, had been transferred to the Philadelphia Division's roster in summer, 1937, for conversion to utility use as the wire grease car.

Although limited c a r s operated through the entire length of Easton, Lehigh Valley Transit Company's policy forbade local passenger accommodations between Centre Square and Seventeenth and Lehigh streets intersection. During World War II limited car traffic increased primarily because workers employed at Bethlehem Steel Company's Bethlehem Plant patronized the comfortable service between Bethlehem and Easton and Bethlehem and Allentown and points enroute. As an added occommodation for steelworkers residing eastward from Bethlehem, the transit company operated the last daily scheduled westbound limited car only as far as the main entrance of the steel plant.

## ELECTRIC INTERURBAN SERVICE
## ABANDONED

With World War II's conclusion most patrons who had patronized limited car service returned to highway travel and the limited car's revenue dwindled accordingly. The transit company replaced electric cars with autobuses in Easton-Bethlehem-Allentown limited service with schedules commencing August 15, 1949. Maintenance crews eventually removed the track between Minsi Trail Junction, Bethlehem, and Centre Square, Easton. During the weeks preceding abandonment of rail

service, Allentown Division's 440 Series city-suburban cars relaced incapacitated 1100 Series cars in limited service. With the cessation of electric interurban service, the transit company transferred the four 1100 Series cars and five utility cars, the sand car having been scrapped earlier, to Allentown Division's roster. The transit company scrapped two passenger cars at Fairview Carbarn and sold two to The Milwaukee Rapid Transit and Speedrail Company, Kenosha, Wisconsin.

Lehigh Valley Transit Company had also conducted high speed freight service between Easton and 69th Street Terminal, Upper Darby, from 1913 until abandonment in 1949. The daily scheduled car, a wooden box type because of clearance problems at Easton freight station, arrived at the station located behind the main carbarn each week day morning and left during midafternoon to become the second car of the Philadelphia-bound freight trip which left Allentown at 7:00 p.m.

Throughout the years of electric car operations the various companies which formed Lehigh Valley Transit Company's Easton Division together either purchased or built one hundred and eighty-two electric cars. One hundred and fifty-three represented single truck passenger cars, nineteen double truck passenger cars, and ten miscellaneous utility cars. Easton Division periodically scrapped obsolete cars: before World War I when the system expanded and required modern cars; following World War I when automobile competition forced curtailment of services; and when the financial depression and continued loss of revenue to highway vehicles forced the system into autobus operations.

END

Lester K. Wismer

Easton-bound car No. 441, an Allentown Division city-suburban car substituting for a disabled 1100 Series car in regular limited service enters Bethlehem's Pembroke section, summer, 1949.

E. Everett Edwards

Snow sweeper No. 1, enroute from Allentown to Easton after being reconditioned, stands on Newton Avenue (Stefko Boulevard), Bethlehem, summer, 1940.

(No. 1, Lewis and Fowler, 1898)

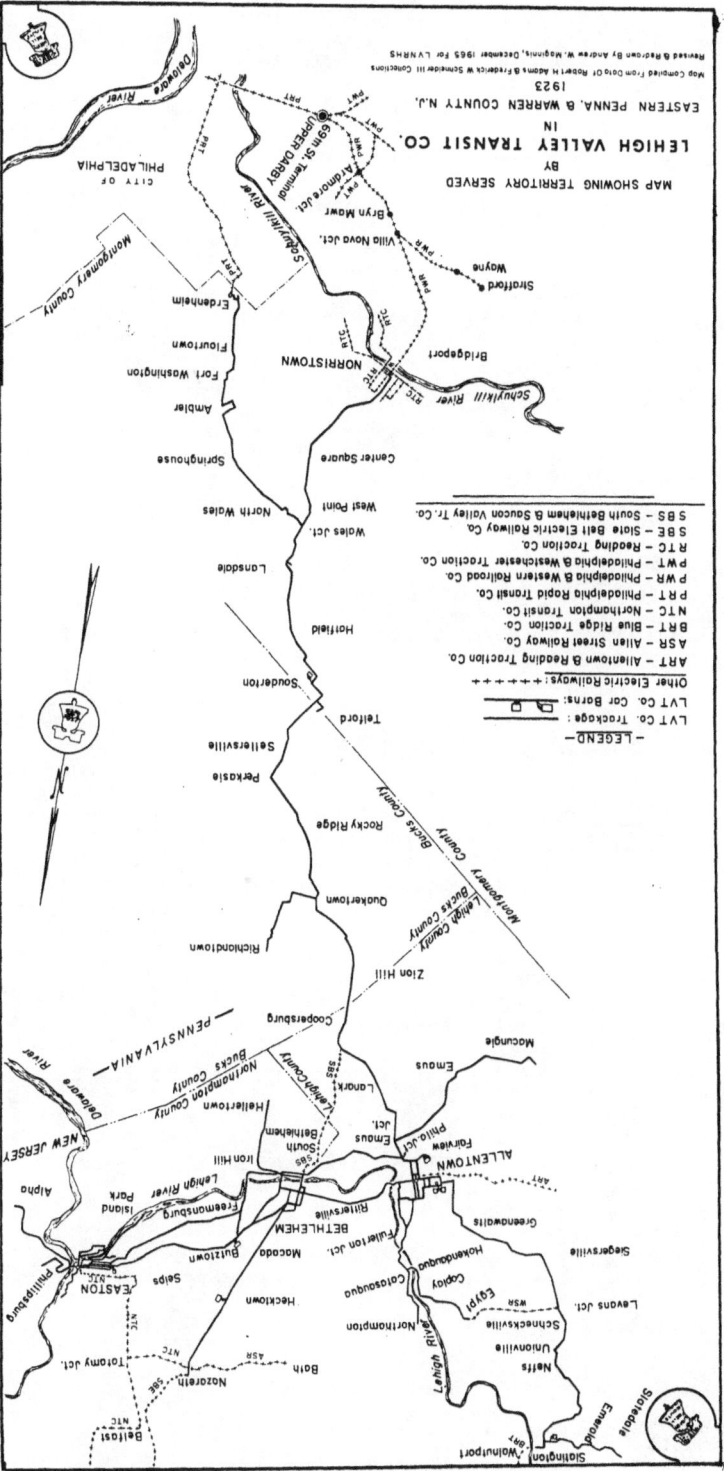

MAP SHOWING TERRITORY SERVED
BY
**LEHIGH VALLEY TRANSIT CO.**
IN
EASTERN PENNA. & WARREN COUNTY N.J.
1923

Map Compiled From Data Of Robert H Adams & Frederick W Schmeider III Collections
Revised & Redrawn By Andrew W. Maginnis, December 1965 For LVRHS

— LEGEND —

LVT Co. Trackage :

LVT Co. Car Barns:

Other Electric Railways: + + + + +

ART – Allentown & Reading Traction Co.
ASR – Allen Street Railway Co.
BRT – Blue Ridge Traction Co.
NTC – Northampton Transit Co.
PRT – Philadelphia Rapid Transit Co.
PWR – Philadelphia & Western Railroad Co.
PWT – Philadelphia & Westchester Traction Co.
RTC – Reading Traction Co.
SBE – State Belt Electric Railway Co.
SBS – South Bethlehem & Saucon Valley Tr. Co.

Delaware River

CITY OF PHILADELPHIA

69th St. Terminal
UPPER DARBY
Ardmore Jct.
Villa Nova Jct.
Bryn Mawr
Stratford
Wayne
Schuylkill River
Montgomery County
Erdenheim
Flourtown
Fort Washington
Ambler
Springhouse
Center Square
NORRISTOWN
Bridgeport
West Point
North Wales
Wales Jct.
Lansdale
Hatfield
Souderton
Telford
Sellersville
Perkasie
Rocky Ridge
Quakertown
Richlandtown
Zion Hill
Coopersburg
Macungie
Emaus
Bucks County
Montgomery County
Lehigh County
PENNSYLVANIA
NEW JERSEY
Delaware River
Alpha
Phillipsburg
EASTON
Lehigh River Park
Island Park
Freemansburg
BETHLEHEM
South Bethlehem
Iron Hill
Hellertown
Lanark
Fairview
Emaus Jct.
Phila. Jct.
ALLENTOWN
Rittersville
Fullerton Jct.
Macada
Butztown
Seips
Hecktown
Northampton
Catasauqua
Hokendauqua
Egypt
Copley
Schnecksville
Siegersville
Greenawalds
Levans Jct.
Neffs
Unionville
Bath
Nazareth
Slatedale
Emerald
Walnutport
Slatington
Northampton County
Lehigh County
Bucks County
Siegfried
Totomy Jct.
Belfast

www.ingramcontent.com/pod-product-compliance
Lightning Source LLC
Chambersburg PA
CBHW030156070426
42447CB00031B/684